Planning for Inquiry

Planning for Inquiry

It's Not an Oxymoron!

Diane Parker
University of Hawai'i

National Council of Teachers of English
1111 W. Kenyon Road, Urbana, Illinois 61801-1096

Excerpt on pages 24 and 25 reprinted with permission of Simon & Schuster Books for Young Readers, an imprint of Simon & Schuster Children's Publishing Division from THE TINY SEED by Eric Carle. Copyright © 1987 Eric Carle Corporation.

Internal photos by Stephen Lum, Gordon Wong, and Diane Parker.

Staff Editor: Bonny Graham
Manuscript Editor: Precision Graphics
Interior Design: Doug Burnett
Cover Design: Precision Graphics
Cover Images: Top: Ariel Skelley/Getty Images
                Bottom: iStockphoto.com/bonniej

NCTE Stock Number: 35600

It is the policy of NCTE in its journals and other publications to provide a forum for the open discussion of ideas concerning the content and the teaching of English and the language arts. Publicity accorded to any particular point of view does not imply endorsement by the Executive Committee, the Board of Directors, or the membership at large, except in announcements of policy, where such endorsement is clearly specified.

Every effort has been made to provide current URLs and email addresses, but because of the rapidly changing nature of the Web, some sites and addresses may no longer be accessible.

Library of Congress Cataloging-in-Publication Data

Parker, Diane.
   Planning for inquiry : it's not an oxymoron! / Diane Parker.
     p. cm.
   Includes bibliographical references.
   ISBN 978-0-8141-3560-0 ((pbk))
  1. Inquiry-based learning. 2. Active learning. 3. Education,
Elementary--Curricula. I. National Council of Teachers of English. II. Title.
LB1027.23.P37 2007
372.139--dc22
                                          2007009626

In Loving Memory of My Parents,
Alfred and Celia Fichman,
         and their gifts of
                 love,
                 learning,
                 and love of learning.

And for Diane Matsuoka,
Person and Principal Extraordinaire,
         who enabled and encouraged me to live my beliefs about learning in
         my classroom.

Contents

Foreword

Diane Stephens
University of South Carolina

I have been lucky in life. Among other things, I have had several great teachers. Diane Parker is one of those teachers. I first met her when I moved to Hawai'i in 1992 and asked around for the names of strong teachers in whose classrooms I could place my undergraduate students for their field experience. I began to learn from Diane as soon as we met. She is a quiet, deeply caring, insightful, and compassionate teacher whose heart and mind touch all the students in her room and all the people in her life. I learned from what Diane did in her classroom, and how and why she did it, and so did our undergraduates.

I learned from and with Diane in other contexts as well. I learned from her as she worked to make mathematics in her classroom not a subject but a tool for inquiry ("Portraits of Susie: Matching Curriculum, Instruction, and Assessment") and as she made connections between the process of learning math and the process of learning language. I learned from Diane when she wrote a book about one of her students, Jamie. As I watched her write and rewrite, working to capture all that was Jamie, it was clear that her passion for learning was exceeded only by her deep love and caring for each and every child. I learned from Diane too as part of a learning community that focused on helping children one on one. Her story about Mayra details the path she took in helping Mayra achieve success as a reader. Diane's narrative also provides a close look into the thinking of a teacher whose heart and soul live in inquiry.

If I had one regret, it would have been that, because Hawai'i is so far from the rest of the United States, only those of us who lived there were able to spend time with Diane as a teacher and as a learner. Imagine my great surprise, then, when I was asked by NCTE to review a book written by Diane Parker. I smiled at the title, smiled all the way through—deeply pleased that Diane had opened the door to her classroom and made it possible for teachers all across the country to visit. By going public with some of the wisdom she has gained through her many years of living a life of inquiry, Diane has given teachers everywhere a wonderful gift.

I want to hand this book to the undergraduates I currently work with and say, "This is what professionalism looks like and sounds like. This is what it means to live your professional life as one who is never content with what one knows, one who is always searching and so, as a consequence, reaches the higher ground many of us only dream of."

And I want to hand it to all the teachers I know—preservice and inservice—and tell them that in this book a very good classroom teacher has demystified "best practice" and shown us all, up close and in detail, what it means to teach deeply and well and to touch the lives of children.

In the field of literacy education, we often talk about knowing children as readers, as well as writers and mathematicians and scientists. In the classroom, Diane Parker lives her life in all these ways and helps her students live in all these ways as well. Her book is a glimpse into that world—a glimpse that will help all of us better understand what it means to be an inquiring teacher, what it means to take an inquiry stance, and what it means to use inquiry to position ourselves and children as lifelong learners. Diane accomplishes this through a book that is magically practical. It is a book that shows us how she thinks and plans and how things work out and sometimes don't work out. It is a book that helps *us* think about how *we* might think and how *we* might plan and what *we* might do to have things work out and what *we* might do when they do not. Like her classroom and like Diane herself, this book is grand and wise and generative and helpful.

Thank you, Diane, for this sharing. You write that "learning must go beyond simply understanding a concept or issue. It must result in action to make the world better." You accomplished that goal as a teacher and as a writer, and this book helps many other teachers do the same.

References

Parker, Diane. *Jamie: A Literacy Story.* Portsmouth, NH: Stenhouse, 1997.

———. "Mayra." *Assessment as Inquiry: Learning the Hypothesis-Test Process.* Ed. Diane Stephens and Jennifer Story. *Assessment as Inquiry.* Urbana, IL: National Council of Teachers of English, 2000. 58–85.

Parker, Diane L., and Anthony J. Picard. "Portraits of Susie: Matching Curriculum, Instruction, and Assessment." *Teaching Children Mathematics* 3 (1997): 376–82.

Preface

There are some things you need to know as you're reading this book. My timing in writing it hasn't been the best. When I started it, I was teaching at Waikele Elementary, the school described in these pages and in which all these classroom stories and events took place; but I didn't finish it until after I retired, and that created a problem.

Waikele Elementary is in a medium-sized suburban town on the island of Oʻahu, Hawaiʻi. Our student population is socioeconomically and ethnically diverse. At the time I taught there, about 40 percent of our students received free or reduced-price lunches and 14 percent were from families whose primary language was not English. All classes were self-contained and heterogeneously grouped, and all included special education students and English language learners. Teachers and students remained together for two- or three-year loops, enabling us to develop a strong sense of community, spiral the curriculum, and build conceptual understandings.

I taught at Waikele for six years, from the day it opened in 1998 until I retired in 2004, working mostly with grades 1, 2, 3, and 4. Those years were by far the most fulfilling of my professional career. Our school was a place where teachers and students could learn and grow together, where learning and learners flourished. I write about my classroom in this book because I know the details of those stories the best; but you could walk into classrooms throughout the school and find similar stories everywhere.

Although I've retired, I'm still connected with my school on a professional level. In my current position with the University of Hawaiʻi College of Education, I supervise preservice teachers who are placed at Waikele. I still see wonderful teaching and learning going on in the classrooms I visit, but the curricular freedoms we once had are eroding and the school I once knew is becoming a different place. Teachers and students are overwhelmed, drowning in an impossible number of standards and benchmarks and a ridiculous number of mandated assessments that seem to be solely for the purpose of reporting data, not for helping kids. Key curricular positions have been eliminated, or their roles changed, so that the level of close collaboration that was vital to inquiries such as the Hidden Places Project (see Chapter 4) is no longer possible. There seems to be less and less time, and less and less support, for what really matters in the classroom. Waikele Elementary, like schools all over the country, is a victim of the stranglehold that the federal government has placed on education.

And that's where the problem of my timing comes in. Given what is happening to our schools, I wondered if I should even bother to finish the book. I wasn't sure if teachers would be able to use it even if they wanted to. But many supportive people convinced me otherwise. As they said, teachers, preservice teachers, and others involved with education need to see what school can be so they can continue to imagine what might be possible. Otherwise, there'll be nothing left but scripts and packaged programs.

So I offer this glimpse of what we once had, with my hope that it's not too late to regain what has been lost. My deepest appreciation to NCTE for their support; and to my wonderful colleagues and friends at Waikele Elementary, with my admiration for their courage in trying to keep inquiry alive against incredible odds. I hope they, and teachers everywhere, will continue to take a stand for meaningful learning. The future of education is truly at stake.

Acknowledgments

Judith Lindfors sees inquiry as an attempt to elicit the help of others in going beyond one's own present understanding (ix). By that definition, there is no doubt that the writing of this book, and everything that has led to it, have been acts of inquiry. Of the countless people who have helped me to go beyond, I'd like especially to thank those who have nudged and supported me in the direction this particular book has taken:

Diane Matsuoka, founding principal of Waikele Elementary, who provided the vision, guidance, climate, and space for learning that made the described events possible. Diane, you are truly one of a kind, and I still believe that education—and the world—would be much better off if we could clone you.

The University of Hawai'i preservice teachers I've mentored, who asked me, "How did you get from X to Y with your students? How do you plan?" Your wondering (probably *bewilderment* would be a more accurate term) forced me to begin trying to figure it out, for myself as well as for all of you.

Tony Picard, University of Hawai'i mathematics professor, whose teaching helped me fit the last piece of the curriculum puzzle in place for myself, and whose suggestion that I examine my curricular decision-making process led to ideas that ultimately became part of this book. Tony, you may recognize elements of the Tasks Study and my "Search for Good Questions" in these pages.

Diane Stephens, whose University of Hawai'i language and literacy courses have always been models of inquiry, and with whom I've had the opportunity to collaborate on a number of projects that have contributed so much to my learning. Hawai'i's loss has definitely been South Carolina's gain. Diane, we miss you, but you're still an inspiration from afar.

Phyllis and David Whitin, who, through their writings and our conversations, have given me inspiration, information, and encouragement. I continue to learn from you both.

Diane Stephens, Phyllis and David Whitin, and two other unidentified individuals, whose thoughtful and constructive reviews of this manuscript helped me take many different perspectives into account as I revised and clarified the original draft. Reviewing manuscripts is no easier than writing them in the first place, and I truly appreciate the care you put into this difficult task. Your professionalism goes far beyond the call.

Gordon Wong and Ben Meyer, whose collaboration made the Hidden Places Project not just possible, but even richer than I had dreamed it might be. How fortunate that we ended up at the same school at the same time! I know you'll both continue to provide the best for your students in whatever capacity you serve them.

Neil Pateman, University of Hawai'i mathematics professor, whose name appears in the accounts of some of the inquiries described in this book, and who has helped my class with many other inquiries over the years as well. Your expertise and your willingness to explore with us have enhanced my students' understanding and appreciation of mathematics in countless ways.

My students at Waikele Elementary School, whose curiosity and spirit made teaching such a joy every day. May you always ask questions and love learning.

My colleagues at Waikele Elementary School, who are the best group of teachers I've ever known and had the privilege to work with. I am heartened by knowing that you are trying to hold fast to what matters in the classroom, and I applaud your courage in doing so. You are constant proof that knowledgeable teachers can still make a difference.

Debora and Stephen Lum, who prepared the chart photographs in these pages, and who devoted so much time and thought to getting them "just right." Deb, thank you also for the conversations over the past eight-plus years, and for asking the hard questions that have pushed my thinking and helped me to understand better what it is I'm thinking.

Zarina Hock and Kurt Austin of NCTE, who took a chance on this book and supported its development and production. If nothing else, at least I've been able to spout my two cents' worth, and for that I'm most grateful.

Bonny Graham, Amy Campbell, Kirsten Dennison, Jennifer Wasson, Cari Rich, and the rest of the editorial and production staff at NCTE and Precision Graphics, whose accessibility and meticulous attention to detail helped this book become a reality. It was a great comfort to know my manuscript was in such capable and caring hands.

And finally, but most of all, my husband, Hoyt, whose support and patience during my long months of work on this manuscript have known no bounds. Hoyt, I'm so thankful you are my partner, in life, love, and learning. Thank you for always helping me to go beyond.

Prologue

T his book grew from many needs. As an elementary teacher trying to explain my rather unconventional classroom to a wide variety of visitors, I've sought in vain to find a book I could hand them that would do the job. It took me a long time to realize that the book I'd been seeking was probably in my head, not on a shelf somewhere, and that if I wanted it I'd have to write it.

This need to explain is twofold: first, to answer those genuine questions about how inquiry works in my classroom; and second, to dispel the myths and misconceptions that exist both within and outside our profession that inquiry means "You don't plan—you just let the kids do what they want." That is simply not true! An inquiry-based curriculum involves constant, complex planning, but it's a different kind of planning that's not necessarily visible on the surface.

There are some wonderful published resources on inquiry, many of which I turn to for guidance and inspiration (see Bibliography). But much of what I've found focuses more on what happens in the classroom: what the kids and teachers *do*. What seems to be harder to find is a more detailed discussion of what the teacher *thinks*: How does the teacher make the decisions that move an inquiry-based curriculum along?

Visitors to my classroom have often told me that they feel I have an intuitive ability to offer learning experiences that foster and sustain my students' inquiries, and they are always curious about how I plan. As I thought about their questions, I began to wonder more myself: Is it just intuition guiding me? Or are there other factors involved? My curiosity led me to do some studies in which I examined my decision-making process in order to inform and improve my teaching.

What I learned has been helpful to me and to others with whom I've shared. But I don't share it as an expert, rather as a learner who is still on a journey to figure it all out. So I don't think of this as a "how-to" book; I prefer to call it a "what if?" book. It offers a framework for thinking through a multitude of possibilities for both short-term and long-term planning, and I'll give examples of both. Keep in mind, though, that it's not a prescription, not a rigid formula; it's simply one way of thinking, one framework, that I hope might serve as a useful springboard for your own curricular explorations.

I hope this book will give some practical, yet theoretically sound, help to those who've asked me the questions they ask themselves: How can I carry out an inquiry-based curriculum in my classroom? How do I get started? How do I recognize, nurture, and sustain the inquiries that do arise? And how can I do this while remaining accountable to mandated curricula, standards, and programs?

There are those who would have us believe that teachers need to follow a script in order to teach effectively. If you've sought out this book, you know the damage that has already been inflicted on our students and on us as professionals in the name of "scientific" research, and you know that true learning can never occur from such a simplistic, one-size-fits-all approach.

Teaching can never be an exact science; students and teachers are individuals, unique unto themselves and to their particular social and cultural contexts. Teachers are the ones who know our students best; *we* need to be the decision-makers in our classrooms. I hope this book will help teachers maintain the confidence and courage to take a stand for the rich, meaningful learning our children deserve. I have enormous faith in the power we have as informed professionals to make a difference in the lives of children. If this book can help in some small way toward that effort, I will be very grateful.

1 What Is Inquiry?

Think of something you're good at: your job, a hobby, special interest, any-thing. How did you learn it? How did you get good at it? What made you want to keep learning it?

Then think of something you're not good at (or think you're not good at). How did you feel when you were trying to learn that? Why did you stop working to learn it? What conditions would have to be present for you to try it again?

Inquiry is a way of looking at the world, a questioning stance we take when we seek to learn something we don't yet know. And when we are truly inquiring about that something, whatever it may be, we drive ourselves to learn more and more because we are seeking answers to our own questions.

An inquiry-based curriculum is a "back-to-basics" curriculum in the truest sense of the phrase. It's based on a fundamental belief about learning and about what it means to be educated. It's thinking back to how learning occurs and how knowledge is created in the first place.

I'll begin with a personal example. I've always enjoyed cooking and baking, and although I don't do much baking nowadays (it's not as much fun since cholesterol became a household word), my family and friends have always appreciated the results of my efforts. But my alleged proficiency didn't happen just by chance; it happened because of a lifelong personal inquiry.

My mom was a great cook, as was my grandmother. Grandma made incredible pastries, all from recipes she had brought from her native Austria and which lived only in her head. One of my earliest memories is of watching her roll out the dough for her apple strudel. Even as a very young child, I marveled at how she stretched that dough until it covered the entire surface of the table and even hung over the edges, looking just like a tablecloth. I was mesmerized; I couldn't figure out how she kept the thickness so even and how she kept the dough from tearing in the process. I wanted to know how she did it, but even more, I wanted to be able to do that myself.

I don't remember asking her to teach me, but I suppose I did, or at least my actions showed my desire to learn. In any event, whenever Grandma or Mom baked, I was at their sides, watching and copying them, working with my own little ball of dough or portion of batter and filling the child-sized pans they had bought me.

As time went on and I became able to work more independently in the kitchen, I grew eager to experiment with other recipes, including those I saw in cookbooks. The kitchen became my laboratory, where I could explore to my heart's content. Sadly, Grandma was gone by then, but Mom was there as my mentor and consultant. She had only one rule: I could make as big a mess as necessary, but I had to clean it all up when I was done.

My explorations resulted in many more failures than successes, especially at first, but I don't remember ever being scolded or punished for those failures. Mom always told me they were part of my learning. She would offer help and tips for future reference, but she never made me feel foolish for not doing things right. She said it was okay just to throw away the disasters that were inedible, but that sometimes what we thought was a disaster might turn out to be good after all, possibly even better than the original—and that many "new," and even famous, recipes were probably created by accident, in much the same way. I suspect that has influenced my belief that we don't need always to follow someone else's recipe, in life as well as in baking.

When I became a newlywed in charge of my own kitchen, I needed and wanted to learn much more about cooking. I read scores of cookbooks, apprenticed myself to other family members and friends, attended cooking demonstrations and classes, and tried out hundreds of recipes on my patient husband, who managed (and still manages) to endure tactfully even my worst attempts at producing something reasonably fit to eat. And in time, my cooking did get better, although I've long since accepted the fact that I'll never be able to make Grandma's strudel. Unfortunately, that art and recipe went with her. But the good news is that Mom managed to preserve many of Grandma's other recipes by observing her as she cooked, converting the amounts of ingredients she used into standard measurements, and writing it all down. Years later, I did the same thing with Mom, recording the recipes for the dishes she made that we loved. And I've even created a few recipes of my own, sometimes intentionally and sometimes by accident, as Mom had said might happen.

The Learning Process

So how did my knowledge of cooking and baking develop? How did it become a passion, rather than a necessary chore? And why, even years later, is it something that still interests me? Let's examine my learning process.

It started with my *wondering,* my *wanting to know:* How in the world could Grandma stretch that dough so magically? And how could her work with that dough have such delicious results?

Because I wanted to know, I *watched, asked questions, helped,* and *explored independently.*

As I tried more and more recipes and met with some success, I was driven to know more, so I *asked more questions, sought more information,* and *continued my independent explorations,* which go on even today.

This, "in a nutshell," is inquiry: You wonder about something and you want to know it—in fact, you're driven to know it because it's intriguing, puzzling, fascinating, and/or personally meaningful to you. You want to move beyond your current understanding. So you set about trying to learn more about that something, and the more you learn, the more questions you have, the more you want to know. It's a continuous cycle: the wondering, the persistence, the satisfaction of finding out, and the new wondering that follows.

Often, you may not find an answer to your initial question, the one that started the inquiry; but that question can lead you to a world of new questions, and that is its primary importance. I never learned how to make strudel like my grandma did; but my wondering about it began my lifetime journey into the culinary world. As Judith Lindfors says of inquiry, "Exploring, not answering, is central" (208).

Conditions for Learning

Inquiry is learning in its most natural and powerful form; and when this type of learning occurs, it can enrich and transform lives. But it's much more likely to lead to in-depth knowledge when certain conditions are in place. Let's look at how Grandma and Mom contributed to my learning, for it could not have progressed as it did without their support:

> They *demonstrated* their art and their love of that art.
>
> They *allowed* and *encouraged* me to watch, help, and try things for myself.
>
> They provided me with *tools* and *assistance.*
>
> They *answered my questions* and *pointed me to further resources* as the need arose.
>
> They provided a *safe environment;* I knew that any "mistakes" were a natural part of my learning and that I wouldn't be scolded for them.

These were the critical elements that kept me going and enabled my continued progress.

Brian Cambourne names these conditions for learning:

Immersion—learners have opportunities for learning and doing in a context that is real and meaningful;

Demonstration—learners see modeling by competent mentors;

Engagement—learners have opportunities to try out challenging tasks;

Expectation—learners feel that adults expect them to be successful;

Responsibility—learners are allowed to make decisions and choices to further their learning;

Employment—learners are offered sufficient time and appropriate contexts for practice;

Approximation—learners' attempts, even less successful ones, are accepted as part of their learning process;

Response—learners receive non-threatening feedback, encouragement, and support toward their further development.

Take a few minutes at this point to match these conditions for learning to places in my cooking narrative. Where do you see the fit? Then reflect on these essentials with regard to your own life and learning, as you look back at this chapter's introductory questions. Do you see the same underlying elements? What else do you see?

The Essence of Inquiry

What I've described so far is an inquiry into learning about and doing a specific something: in this case, cooking and baking. But can this process work with deeper inquiries, those dealing with more complex issues and with questions that may not have answers? I'd respond by saying that the most important questions in the world don't have simple or readily apparent answers, or even any answers at all, yet philosophers, historians, mathematicians, scientists, and others spend their lives searching for knowledge, wisdom, and enlightenment.

My work with children has taught me that they, too, are philosophers, historians, mathematicians, scientists, and deep thinkers about their world. They wonder about weighty issues and ask profound questions. The problem is that adults may dismiss or trivialize the questions they do hear, sending the message that those questions aren't important. Yet if we want our students to think deeply, our first job is to find out what they're wondering about, to help them see that their questions are indeed important, and to help them connect their search for knowledge and wisdom with that of others. When we do this, we often find that the questions they ask can be the most powerful and effective ways to approach curriculum. We can address even mandated topics more effectively if we begin with our students. I'll share specific examples in later chapters.

It all boils down to the quality of learning we desire for those we are charged to educate. Do we want them simply to memorize facts and procedures in order to pass a test? Or do we want them to *want* to know, to seek to know, and ultimately, to understand themselves and their world more deeply as a result of their knowing? Is it enough that they can recite the dates and locations of wars, or is it more important that their inquiries lead them to look more closely into how and why wars occur and to envision how things might be different? Should they just know how to read charts and graphs, or should they learn how to interpret, evaluate, and even question the data they're looking at in light of what it purports to show?

All too often, school is seen as a place where students passively receive what someone else has arbitrarily classified as "knowledge"— what Alfie Kohn refers to as "bunch o' facts" models (*What to Look For* 94). However, when we reflect on how people learn naturally, and the difference in the depth of that learning, we can see the contrast. Covering a topic by memorizing key aspects of it can perhaps help us pass a test; but truly inquiring into a topic, by pursuing answers to our own questions, can help us change ourselves and, perhaps, our world. This is the essence of inquiry: Inquiry is learning itself, a way of trying to make sense of our lives and experiences. And it's the stance we want our students to take with regard to all their thinking, learning, and living, not just at a particular time of day.

Herein, of course, lies the challenge. How can an inquiry approach fit within the required curriculum, with its mandated content and multiple subject areas? It's possible only if we think of curriculum organization in a different way. Traditionally, each subject area has been structured according to the ways people have categorized its generally accepted knowledge base through the perspectives of their own disciplines. But this has been done for convenience of organization; knowledge doesn't fit neatly into narrow subject-area boundaries, and neither does inquiry. It's the questions that are the core of inquiry, not the disciplines themselves, and therefore inquiry cuts across all disciplines. Jerome Harste says, "Rather than curriculum being framed in terms of the content areas, the inquiry questions of learners become the organizational device for curriculum. Integration occurs in the head of the learner, rather than in the daily schedule of the teacher" ("What Education as Inquiry" 3–4).

This, then, is where planning for inquiry must begin. If curriculum is to be organized around the genuine questions of learners, then it cannot be organized around predetermined objectives or units within traditional subject-area boundaries. So what does that mean for students and teachers? How are their roles, and their classrooms, different? What might they look like? In the next chapter, I'll talk more about those differences and about ways to get started with inquiry-based planning.

2 Inquiry-Based Planning: How Is It Different? How Can I Get Started?

Most of us were required to do lesson planning as part of our pre-service teacher education. And I'm willing to wager that most of us had to do very similar types of lesson plans. The format might have differed, but essentially, we had to decide on and list our objectives, or what the students would be learning; a planned initiating activity; a step-by-step, detailed plan for the procedures to follow; and a closing, or evaluative, activity. The procedures usually included all the questions we planned to ask, in the order we needed to ask them, and, in some instances, even the expected student responses. I remember how lost and helpless we felt when those responses didn't occur. We had no idea what to say or do next. It's funny to think about it now, but it definitely wasn't funny at the time!

Sadly, it seems that not much has changed with regard to lesson planning in many preservice teacher education programs. It's still all about the teacher. Students have little connection with the lesson except as receivers of what the teacher has planned and delivered. And often, what is delivered is little more than what Diane Stephens refers to as the proverbial "dog and pony show."

I don't argue with the need for teachers to plan. Artful teaching is indeed planful teaching. But planning needs to be consistent with what we know about learning. As our understanding of learning evolves, planning, too, must evolve to incorporate students' interests and wonderings.

Some people mistakenly think inquiry-based teaching involves little or no planning: "Just let them do whatever they want." On the contrary, it involves a huge amount of planning (see Figure 2.1). I spend long hours reading, thinking through possibilities both alone and with others, and gathering materials and resources. You have to be better prepared than ever because you have to be able to respond to children's interests and questions, both anticipated and unanticipated—and believe me, those wonderful, surprising, unanticipated questions will astound you.

Myths about Inquiry	Facts about Inquiry
Inquiry means doing a report.	Inquiry is learning.
Teachers do little or no planning; they just let students do whatever they want.	Teachers do careful planning.
Teachers don't need to know learners, content, or resources; anything goes.	Teachers need to know learners, content, resources, and processes so as to guide inquiry.
Inquiry is an "extra," not part of the established curriculum.	Inquiry is the heart of the curriculum.
With inquiry, you can't meet standards.	With inquiry, you can meet and go beyond standards.

Figure 2.1. Myths and facts about inquiry.

Just listen to some of them—and these are *real* questions from *real* kids: I wonder who invented blankets? I wonder if sea monsters are real? If they had TVs in 1807? If twenty-five elephants can be heavier than the Empire State Building? What does learning mean? Do bugs have souls? How hot is the sun? What would we look like if we didn't have any bones? How does the owl twist its head all around? Do fish get thirsty and what water do they drink if they get thirsty?

Aren't kids' minds amazing? Think about the potential their questions hold for allowing us to take off into experiences and investigations that are open-ended enough to enable each student to enter at his or her own level of development—which is where differentiation comes in. It's okay for them to start wherever they are; they'll continue to refine their understandings as they revisit significant concepts in a variety of different contexts over the years. The possibilities are endless.

The catch, of course, is that you have to know content well, because you have to know where you're going and what you want your students to understand. But that doesn't mean you have to know all the answers to all their questions. You simply need to be a learner along with your students. When you realize that there are infinite ways to get where you want to go, you also realize that your best chance of getting there is to take the journey *with* your students, not to drag them along kicking and screaming behind you. And that means building on their interests and questions, starting with what matters to them and weaving through the curriculum from there. It's a different kind of planning, one that for me is so much more fun and exciting.

Beginning with Students' Questions

Let's look at some quick examples. Suppose I want my students to explore linear measurement. There are countless ways we can address this mathematical concept while meeting their interests. One year, my kids became interested in treasure maps as we read some adventure stories together. So they used measurement to create their own maps to mark the spot where they had buried our Halloween jack-o'-lantern as part of a scientific study of decomposition—and the next spring, they followed those very same maps so they could dig up their "treasure" and find out what had happened to poor Jack.

Another year, the kids wanted to find the shortest route from our classroom to the cafeteria so that one of their classmates who had a broken leg and had to use crutches would be able to navigate more easily. Out came the string, meter sticks and yardsticks, trundle wheels, chalk, and an assortment of child-invented measuring devices, and we were off on a different sort of measurement adventure with an important purpose.

Still another year, one of my first graders asked, "How do you measure something that's bigger than a ruler, if you only have one ruler?" I threw the question back to the class and they worked in pairs to answer it as I watched in amazement. Some kids chose to trace the outline of their ruler over and over on their desktops; others placed the ruler in a more traditional fashion and "eyeballed" their measurements or made markings for accuracy; still others cut string to fit their desktops and attempted to see how many times it would wrap around the ruler. There were as many different solutions as there were pairs of children, all learning more about measurement because of this wonderful question that I'd never have thought of myself—but you can believe I've used that question with many other classes since then!

Here's one of my favorite measurement stories: My student teacher, Kim Min, was required to plan a unit on measurement for her mathematics methods course, but she wanted to link it to our first graders' interests. Kim and I brainstormed several possibilities for incorporating measurement, but none of them seemed exactly "right." Meanwhile, the class had been studying about outer space and the students were preparing to share their learning with each other. Kim asked them, "What makes a good presentation?" She had thought the kids would say things like, "Speak clearly," "Look at the audience," or "Know your material," and she was not at all surprised when some of those thoughts emerged. But then one child said, and the rest enthusiastically agreed, "To have a good presentation, you need a stage!" (You never know what kids are thinking!) Kim realized immediately that this was the opportunity she was looking for: To explore measurement, the kids would build a stage! And so they did. They spent the next several weeks planning and building. They learned how to measure the available area, create and evaluate blueprints and scale models (first-grade versions), and finally, to choose and build the finished product. The collaboration and decision making involved in the process were invaluable as well, and the satisfaction they gained from actually using their creation for their presentations was immeasurable. The stage remained in our classroom and was well used for both formal and informal events throughout the rest of the school year.

I hope the above examples have helped to show what I mean about how we can link the students' interests to worthwhile learning in any number of ways. In each of these four different experiences, the kids were exploring linear measurement, but they were doing so in the context of a problem that mattered to them. When the interest is there, the learning will follow.

Listening to Students' Wonderings

Sometimes we can gain insight into students' thinking, and generate ideas for curriculum, by doing a bit of eavesdropping. One day, I overheard this conversation among a group of my first graders:

> *Kaeo:* Who invented the period?
>
> *Jon:* Maybe someone was accidentally running and the pencil point made a dot.
>
> *Ire:* Maybe they dropped their pencil and made a dot.
>
> *Tavana:* Maybe George Washington invented it.
>
> *Kaeo:* Maybe Jesus, when he got bigger and thought about it.
>
> *Tasha:* Maybe God invented it.
>
> *Kaeo:* Maybe it was made of rain. God looked at the water and saw little tiny dots.
>
> *Tavana:* Maybe he couldn't read the words. They got all squooshed up.
>
> *Ire:* Maybe he made a dot on paper and said, "Oh yeah, that could be a period."
>
> *Brittany:* It's good thing. If we didn't have (periods), it wouldn't make sense.

I was completely taken with this discussion, not just because they were talking about punctuation—which I had not expected would be the topic of their conversation at all—but because of what they were asking about it. Even though these students already knew what a period is and how it's used, they had now begun to wonder about how it came to be and why it exists at all. They were ready to explore the function of periods and other punctuation at a deeper level, and I took full advantage of the opportunity. Over the next several weeks, we compared text excerpts written with and without punctuation, and the effects of each on readers trying to comprehend them; we noticed and explored the way punctuation is used in a variety of texts; and I invited the kids to try using punctuation marks they had never used before or in ways they had never tried before, and to share with the rest of us. As a result, many of them not only expanded their repertoire of punctuation use, but they began to use punctuation much more intentionally, bringing more clarity to their writing, and they began to gain more meaning from the texts they read as well. For these students, punctuation had become much more than a bunch of symbols; it had become theirs, to own and to use.

Punctuation is taught as part of every first-grade curriculum, so if we look at it from that standpoint, we could say I had met that requirement just by introducing it to them in the first place, and I could have left it at that. But I believe they gained much more by going into it so much further, and I also gained much more from listening to them. As with the ruler question, I've used some version of this "Who invented the period?" question with many other classes I've worked with in the years that followed.

On another occasion (with a different first-grade class), Aaron wondered aloud while working with a group in the block corner: "Who invented numbers?" This conversation ensued:

Jason: The factory made it with the machines.

Bret: He [Jason] means the page with numbers on it.

Aaron: Not by the factory. Who was the first to imagine numbers?

Nick: I think God made the numbers because God made everything except the houses.

Jason: I don't think so, because God just takes care of the dead people.

Bret: Then how did we get born? And how did our parents come?

Jessica: God makes us first, and then we grow older.

Samantha: But we're talking about numbers. God put numbers in their brain.

Aaron: God passed it on to everyone he knew and they told everyone else.

Keone: I think numbers came from China, because I know they invented fireworks so maybe they invented numbers.

Brian: I think the governor made numbers. He was the first one alive.

Susie: People was born and found work that said numbers and told to the whole world.

Samantha: They would think about how many animals or dinosaurs they killed.

Susie: How old they are and when their birthday is.

Brandy: They maybe had a little bit of stuff and wanted more.

Elena: For kids to learn.

As I listened, it seemed to me that the natural next step would be to investigate Aaron's question since so many of the kids had already become involved in his inquiry. So I took them to the school library to look for information about the origins of number systems, and we invited Neil Pateman, mathematics professor at the University of Hawai'i, to visit our classroom and talk with us further. As with the punctuation question, I was learning that kids think about things much more deeply than we often give them credit for, and that they're ready and eager to tackle questions of this nature. Are such questions important enough to spend time on, even if they're not "on the test"? That's something we need to decide for ourselves. Personally, I see these overheard conversations as gifts handed to us by our students. They're telling us what they want to learn; how can we pass up such opportunities and still call ourselves teachers?

The Unexpected Curriculum

Our students are truly our best teachers. They've helped me see that it's not enough to think of curriculum as simply covering material and teaching concepts, and this is the view of curriculum I'm sharing here. I'm not talking about scope and sequence charts, sets of ready-made lesson plans, or curriculum maps organized around pre-planned content areas, focused studies, or "essential" questions. There are already many resources available with that kind of information, and I find it useful to consult them for suggested learning engagements that might fit with my kids' inquiries. But planning for inquiry is not pre-planning for inquiry, and I hope to show the difference in this book. I want to offer a way to uncover the unexpected curriculum that can evolve as you consider kids' questions with a "what if?" frame of mind and with an acceptance of the uncertainties that are a part of it. You can't know ahead of time which way it will go and you have to be okay with that. Harste says, "If inquiry is truly inquiry, it must be open. No one can predetermine the outcomes. This is really the difference between 'discovery learning' as a curricular model and inquiry" ("Inquiry-Based Instruction" 3). David and Phyllis Whitin agree: "We recognize inquiry not as a question or activity but as a perspective on learning that celebrates surprise, thrives on doubt, and flourishes in tension. . . . This is a productive tension that encourages us all to make connections and forge unforeseen possibilities. It is a tension that keeps us all young in heart and mind. It keeps us growing and learning" (*Inquiry at the Window* 143).

Inquiry-based planning is truly an inquiry in itself. By its very nature, it has to be. Just as an inquiry-based curriculum revolves around the questions of students, inquiry-based planning revolves around the questions of teachers as they consider their students' questions. It seems self-evident to me now, but it was only through reflecting on my planning process that I was able to come to that realization. And it was only through reflecting on that realization that I could begin to see more clearly the differences between this process and more traditional types of planning (see Figure 2.2).

As I plan for inquiry in my classroom, there are questions that continually drive my thinking and influence the decisions I make. Some of them are:

- How can I help my students to realize that they have questions and that their questions matter?
- How can I create a classroom environment that supports my students' inquiries without directing them?
- How can I help my students connect their inquiries to questions and issues of deeper personal and social significance?
- How can I help my students share their learning in interesting, relevant, authentic ways? But—how can I help them see that learning is the point, not giving a report or getting a grade?

The teacher's role in inquiry-based planning is considerable. You have to know learners, learning, and content, and you have to continually try to link these in ways that will enable your students to learn. "The role of the teacher in an inquiry-based curriculum is to possess not only expert knowledge about different disciplines but also expert knowledge about how learners learn" (Berghoff, Egawa, Harste, and Hoonan 87). It's a daunting task, but the good thing is that as you learn more about and with your students, you get better at it.

Traditional Planning	Inquiry-Based Planning
Starts with teacher-directed topics and lessons.	Starts with students' wonderings and wanting to know.
Organized by established disciplines, predetermined objectives.	Organized around questions of learners.
Teacher preplans unit so knows all steps ahead of time.	Because unit is not preplanned, teacher can't know all steps ahead of time.
Teacher selects all resources and activities.	Students have choice in selecting resources and activities.
Decisions about "what to do next" are made by writers of publishers' manuals.	Decisions about "what to do next" are made by teacher and students.
Teacher directs instruction, students follow.	Teacher supports and guides learning.
Covers only required curriculum.	Allows for unexpected curriculum.
Study is "finished" when topic covered.	New questions can keep inquiry going over time.

Figure 2.2. Traditional v. inquiry-based planning.

Getting Started: A Fishing Expedition

Teachers often ask me, "How do you know where to begin?" My answer is, "I don't know." You can't know where your students' interests lie if you don't know your students yet. So I start each school year with what I call a "fishing expedition." I watch, I listen, and I throw out bait based on what I see and hear. Sometimes I hook them right away, but most often, I have to keep trying for a while.

For example, I might overhear a question the kids are discussing among themselves, and I decide to throw that question back at them and see where it will lead. Sometimes, as with the punctuation or "Who invented numbers?" questions, we can take off immediately. But more often than not, the discussion will fall flat and I'll think to myself, "Well, that didn't go anywhere." Most of the time, that happens because the question had an answer that was simple and quick to obtain, such as, "What does the inside of a cocoa bean look like?" Once you have your answer, there's nowhere else to go with it—unless, of course, you happen to be someone who wants to know everything there is to know about chocolate. (If you're like me and many others, though, you're mostly content just to eat it.)

Some questions don't sustain the kids' interest for other reasons. Perhaps the topic just wasn't what they thought it would be, or the question didn't arise from a real inquiry in the first place. But that's okay. I think these false starts are unavoidable, and, in fact, they're necessary, both to get the process going and to give me an opportunity for trial-and-error insight into what makes each particular group tick.

Even when I do hit on something the kids seem interested in—the first nibble, so to speak—their first inquiries usually don't go far, maybe only lasting a day, an hour, or less. That's okay, too. It's the start of a process, one that may be new to them and that they have to try on for size. What I want is for them to begin to understand that their questions matter and deserve to be explored. The explorations themselves will grow in depth as the kids become comfortable with the process.

I want to make one thing very clear here, in case it's not obvious. While I'm fishing, learning is not standing still. We are engaged in a variety of planned curricular experiences, just as any other class would be. But throughout, I remain constantly on the lookout for that shining opportunity that will enable us to go deeper.

Back to the fishing expedition. Often, the questions we hear kids ask are not necessarily what they really want to know. Lindfors tells a wonderful story about her nine-year-old son. He had heard that the librarians in his community would answer questions by phone, and he was so amazed and curious that he wanted to try calling in a question himself. The question he decided to ask was, "How many teeth does a fox have?" However, when he expressed no further interest in foxes once his question was answered, Lindfors realized that he had used that question merely as a means of getting at his real inquiry. She explains: "He was indeed inquiring. His *question* was about foxes' teeth; his *inquiry* was about librarians (Do librarians answer questions?). He asked the one in order to find out about the other. How often we do this" (125). Reflecting on this and similar experiences, Lindfors began to question herself more about what that difference means to both learner and teacher: "The challenge is to hear through the words to the intention that lies behind them and gives birth to them" (64).

Kathy Short, Jerome Harste, and Carolyn Burke talk about the importance of taking the time to help learners find questions for inquiry. They believe that if students have ample time to explore topics and resources without feeling pressured to start "doing research" immediately, they will find their own connections and move beyond superficial questions to more focused, more significant inquiries (265).

One of the keys to fostering an inquiry-based curriculum is learning to recognize questions that are generative, that offer possibilities for extended investigations and broader connections. It's not necessarily something we do naturally (I didn't), but with conscious effort, it can be learned (I'm still learning). It takes time, effort, patience, and perhaps a bit of luck to uncover learners' real inquiries, but expending that time and effort is critical to the process. There are no "right" or "wrong" inquiry questions. But there are all types of questions, ranging from trivial to profound. As teachers, we need to help kids think more deeply about their world so that their questions will become more and more thoughtful, and we need to develop in ourselves the ability to distinguish the surface inquiries from the underlying ones. But I think it's only through encouraging and developing our students' sense of wonder that any of this can happen. It's the act of wondering, not necessarily the specific questions they're initially asking, that establishes an inquiry mindset and gets the process going.

If you keep on fishing, eventually you'll get more than a nibble; you'll get a bite that will jolt you with its intensity. That's the one you'll want to try to follow (see Chapter 4 for one example). Sometimes, if you're lucky, that one question will take you further than you ever imagined—if you're not afraid to go with it and see where it leads you, even if you don't know ahead of time where that may be (and if it's a true inquiry, you can't know ahead of time). And you can learn how to go with it by asking yourself certain questions throughout the process. That's where having a framework for your observations and decision making can help. In the next chapter, I'll share my version of such a framework.

3 A Responsive/Reflective Planning Framework

We've talked about the "what" and the "why" of inquiry-based planning. Many people agree with the concept, but they find the "how" so nebulous that they give up before they've even tried. I don't pretend that my version of the "how" is the only one, but I share it here with the hope that it will make clear the distinct structure underlying what is not visible on the surface.

As I studied my curricular decision-making process, I recorded and named this framework to help me and the preservice teachers I've worked with. It can be applied to any traditional subject area, but I find it especially helpful for looking at curriculum from an integrated, holistic perspective and for reflecting on my classroom practice.

Responsive/reflective planning is based on what Yetta Goodman calls "kidwatching," which is the foundation of a learner- and learning-centered curriculum. It's a continuous inquiry cycle of watching and listening to students, thinking about how you might link their wonderings to worthwhile learning experiences, and then making your best guess as to how to proceed (see Figure 3.1 and Appendix 1). You then watch and listen again, and on that basis you decide what you might try next. Although you can draw from known, familiar learning experiences, the possibilities for venturing beyond are infinite if you think of those experiences as starting points rather than as complete recipes.

Let's begin by looking at the use of this framework for shorter-term, day-to-day planning. I've illustrated each part of the cycle with a few examples from my classroom. Although each of these particular examples began with a single curricular focus, notice the cross-curricular links that emerged as the inquiries progressed. I'll show this process more explicitly in the long-term example shared in Chapter 4.

After you've read these examples, try generating some possibilities of your own. As you watch and listen to your students, expand your vision and think about how those gems you notice and overhear, and even those unanticipated classroom happenings, can be mined for curricular purposes.

Responsive/Reflective Lesson Planning Framework

Step 1. What do you notice?

Things to consider: What is happening with the students that you might build upon? What classroom events are occurring? What books are the students enjoying? What questions are they asking? What interests are they demonstrating? How do you know?

Step 2. Response: What are some possibilities for building on what you notice?

Things to consider: How might you turn some aspect of Step 1 into a worthwhile educational experience? Consult your standards and other resources and brainstorm some ideas.

Step 3. Choose one idea from Step 2 and develop it further.

Things to consider: What could you have the children do? How will it connect with Step 1 or with previous things they've done? How will it connect with your school's required content and standards?

Step 4. Afterward: Reflection

Things to consider: What happened? How do you feel about it? How do the children feel about it? Was this experience meaningful to them? Did it challenge their thinking? How do you know? What do you think they learned? How do you know? What did *you* learn? What might you do differently next time?

Step 5. Possibilities

Things to consider: What possibilities, if any, do you see for extending this experience further? Go back to Step 1 and brainstorm some ideas.

Figure 3.1. Responsive/reflective lesson planning framework.

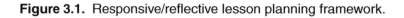

The Framework

Note: I've recorded the steps below in much more detail than I'd normally write as I plan, so that I may share the underlying, detailed thinking process involved.

You will not need to answer every question under every heading every time. The questions are meant to help you focus your thinking, but they won't all apply to every planning situation.

Step 1. What do you notice?

Things to consider: What is happening with the students that you might build upon? What classroom events are occurring? What books are the students enjoying? What questions are they asking? What interests are they demonstrating? How do you know?

Example 1: Some inquiries begin with a direct question. One of my third graders asked me one day, "Is it true you should never begin a sentence with *and*? That's what another teacher once told me." Another student followed with, "What about *but* and *because*?" I asked the rest of the class what they thought, and they all agreed, many of them saying they had been told the same "rule" by their parents or other adults. (Katie Wood Ray reports a similar question from her students in her book, *Wondrous Words* [20]. It seems some language myths are universal.)

Example 2: David and Phyllis Whitin discuss the importance of creating a classroom atmosphere that acknowledges and values surprise as an important part of learning: "if we view learners as respected sense-makers and meaning-makers, then surprise is a very healthy sign; it means that children are trying to make sense of a given situation and explain certain unexpected results" (*Math Is Language Too* 10). Thus, surprise can often launch an exciting and productive inquiry.

My first graders had been learning about the harmful effects of litter on the environment. As part of that study, they had collected, sorted, and counted litter from our school campus. They hadn't expected to find much litter because our campus is relatively clean, so the kids were greatly surprised to have found twenty-four candy wrappers, and they discussed their concern about those findings.

Example 3: Sometimes an inquiry can begin accidentally, in connection with an authentic event or need for information. One day at recess, four of my third-grade boys were caught playing with razor blades. One of the four had sneaked the razor blades to school just to show off, to be a "big shot" with his peers. He wasn't a child who would intentionally hurt anyone, and we knew that, but nevertheless, what he did could have had disastrous consequences if an accident had occurred—and, of course, razor blades are contraband items according to school policy. The teacher on recess duty sent the four boys to the principal, and they received severe consequences for their actions.

Step 2. Response: What are some possibilities for building on what you notice?

Things to consider: How might you turn some aspect of Step 1 into a worthwhile educational experience? Consult your standards and other resources and brainstorm some ideas.

Example 1: I saw this question as an opportunity for the kids to learn more about writers' craft. I hoped that if they spent time looking more closely at the words published authors really use, they'd learn the answer for themselves and, in the process, be able to use this type of crafting technique more intentionally because they'd understand more about writers' decision making.

Example 2: The issue of the candy wrappers presented an opportunity for the kids to translate their concern for their school environment into some specific action that might help make things better. I decided to start by asking them to help brainstorm with me. Do we need to let others know what we found out? If so, how should we let them know?

Example 3: Eventually, the students were forgiven and allowed to return to class. But the problem was not solely theirs; there were other issues that needed to be addressed with the whole class: the fact that the students had disregarded the school rules and the danger their disregard posed to everyone; the silence of some of their classmates who knew about the razor blades but had chosen not to inform any adults; and the four culprits' growing realization that they needed to warn others about what they had done so that no one else would do such a thing. We talked as a class about how we might turn this unfortunate situation into something that could help our whole school.

Step 3. Choose one idea from Step 2 and develop it further.

Things to consider: What could you have the children do? How will it connect with Step 1 or with previous things they've done? How will it connect with your school's required content and standards?

How might you facilitate this plan? What will you do? What questions might you ask? What will you need (information, materials, etc.) to carry it out?

How will this plan fit with what you know or believe about how children learn? How will it fit with what you know or believe about this particular group of students? How will it fit with what you know or believe about yourself as a teacher?

What do you hope the children will gain or learn from this? Why is this important for them? What do *you* hope to learn from this? Why is this important for you?

Example 1: I decided to start by having the students look closely at a number of books in our classroom library and copy onto large charts any sentences they found that began with *and*, *but*, or *because*, and to note the book titles and authors' names for later reference. We could then share and discuss their findings, which I expected would probably surprise many of them and therefore have more of an impact on their learning. Again, I felt it was important for them to see for themselves what published authors really do, to experience a real-life lesson in grammar and usage, rather than simply reading about or memorizing rules that may or may not be accurate or useful.

Example 2: As a result of our discussion, the kids decided they needed to tell the rest of the school about the candy wrappers. They decided to make "reminder" posters and accompanying speeches, which they'd share throughout the school to create wider awareness of the problem.

Example 3: I decided to begin by having each of the students reflect in writing about their individual roles in the incident: Did they know about the razor blades before their classmates got caught? If so, what, if anything, did they do about it and why? If a similar situation occurred in the future, what, if anything, might they do differently and why? These reflections would not be shared with the rest of the class; I wanted the students to feel free to express their honest thoughts without the fear of being embarrassed. I felt they needed to think about their personal responsibilities as members of our learning community, and they needed to write in order to get at what they were really thinking.

Afterward, we met as a whole class, had a general discussion about the issues, and brainstormed ways we might share this incident with the school to warn others of its seriousness. The students decided on a number of things they wanted to do: They'd create posters to place around the school; they'd write and distribute flyers; and they'd create advertising to present on our school's student-produced closed-circuit television news broadcast. They formed committees to begin working on their chosen projects.

Step 4. Afterward: Reflection

Things to consider: What happened? How do you feel about it? How do the children feel about it? Was this experience meaningful to them? Did it challenge their thinking? How do you know? What do you think they learned? How do you know? What did *you* learn? What might you do differently next time?

Example 1: We placed several piles of books on the carpet in our reading area, and students began exploring and charting what they found (see Figure 3.2). They were absolutely amazed to find so many examples of *and, but,* and *because* sentences, especially by so many of their favorite authors.

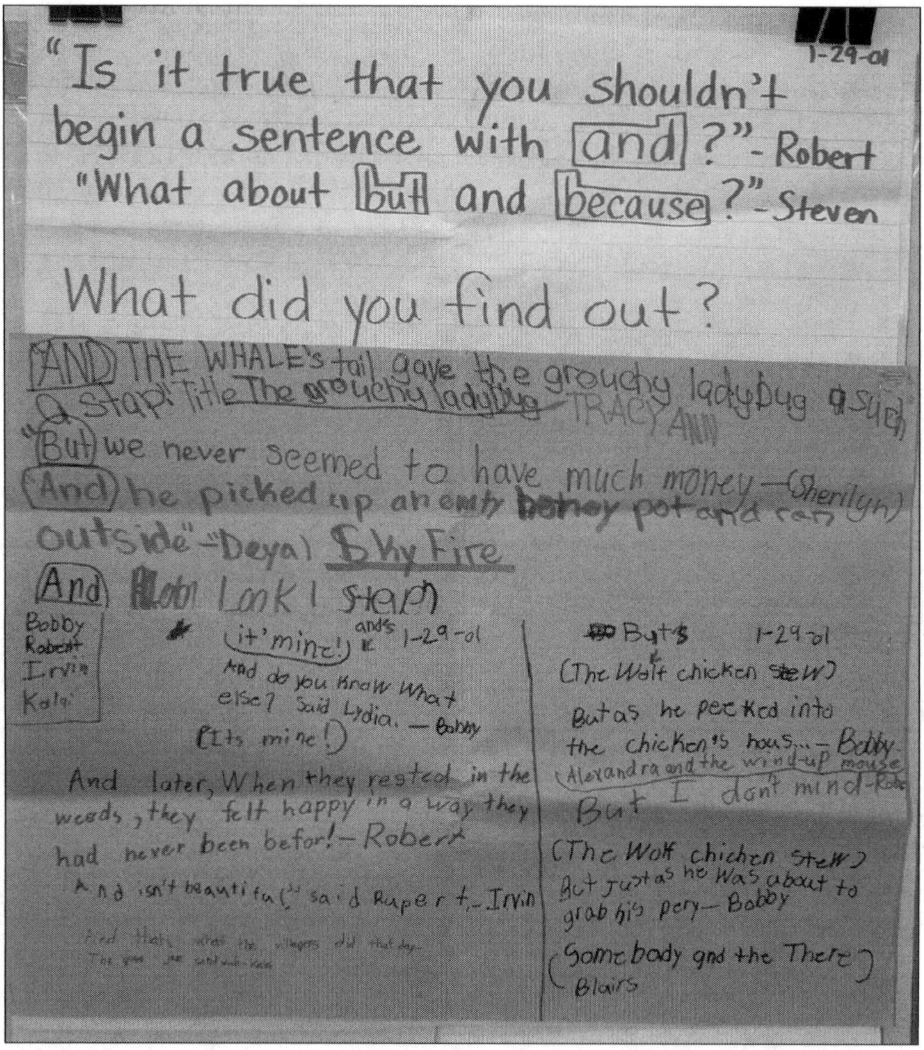

Figure 3.2. Students record *and*, *but*, and *because* sentences by their favorite authors.

When they shared their surprise, I asked them, "What do you think? Authors such as these are well-known, respected writers. Why would they begin so many sentences with these words?" The kids said, "They didn't know the rule!" I asked them, "So where did the rule come from? Who do you think made it?" and that stopped them cold. Finally, after a few minutes of silence, someone said, "Maybe that's not the rule," and I could see the growing puzzlement on their faces.

Figure 3.2 continued

I then asked them, "Whether it's a rule or not, why would authors start their sentences in this way?" They shared, and I charted, a variety of theories. Their ideas began in a more general vein (e.g., "It sounds better." "It sounds more interesting."), but as I probed and they built on each others' thoughts, they grew a bit more specific (e.g., "It's like he's acting it out." "It's like he's using his imagination."). Finally, one student said, "If it's a fact [meaning nonfiction text], maybe you shouldn't do it, but if it's a story, it's good." The class agreed with that observation, so I asked them what makes "it" good in a story, and that led to even closer investigation.

We reviewed the list of theories they had generated and, after further discussion, they agreed that the authors must have made intentional decisions to write their stories in this way, but the kids still weren't quite sure why. I suggested that they might want to test their hypothesis. We copied a few paragraphs from their favorite books, then rewrote the paragraphs without the words in question and compared the effects of each on us as readers. Here's an example, from Eric Carle's *The Tiny Seed* (see Figure 3.3).

As Eric Carle wrote it: "There is another plant that grows much faster than the new little plants. It is a big fat weed. *And* it takes all the sunlight and the rain away from one of the small new plants. *And* that little plant dies.

"The tiny seed hasn't begun to grow yet. It will be too late! Hurry! *But* finally it too starts to grow into a plant" (italics added).

What if Eric Carle wrote it this way? "There is another plant that grows much faster than the new little plants. It is a big fat weed. It takes all the sunlight and the rain away from one of the small new plants. That little plant dies.

"The tiny seed hasn't begun to grow yet. It will be too late! Hurry! Finally it too starts to grow into a plant."

The students' responses to the rewritten paragraphs left them no doubt as to why the authors had written as they did: In their words, "It makes your writing sound more like a story." They saw how flat the text sounded without those small but critical words.

Ray explains that "starting a sentence with 'and' lets the writer set a part of something off by itself—showing it's still tied to the rest (by the 'and') but giving it its own sentence significance" (171). While my students never explained it at that level, they nevertheless noticed, understood, and used that technique intentionally in their writing from that day on.

Example 2: After sharing their posters and speeches, my students expressed the desire to collect and analyze campus litter monthly to see whether their efforts made a difference and to report their findings to the other classes (see Figures 3.4 and 3.5). This provided me with an opportunity to incorporate more mathematics by involving them more deeply in working with data, beginning with paper-and-pencil recording and, with the help of our technology coordinator, Gordon Wong, evolving to the use of age-appropriate computer graphing programs.

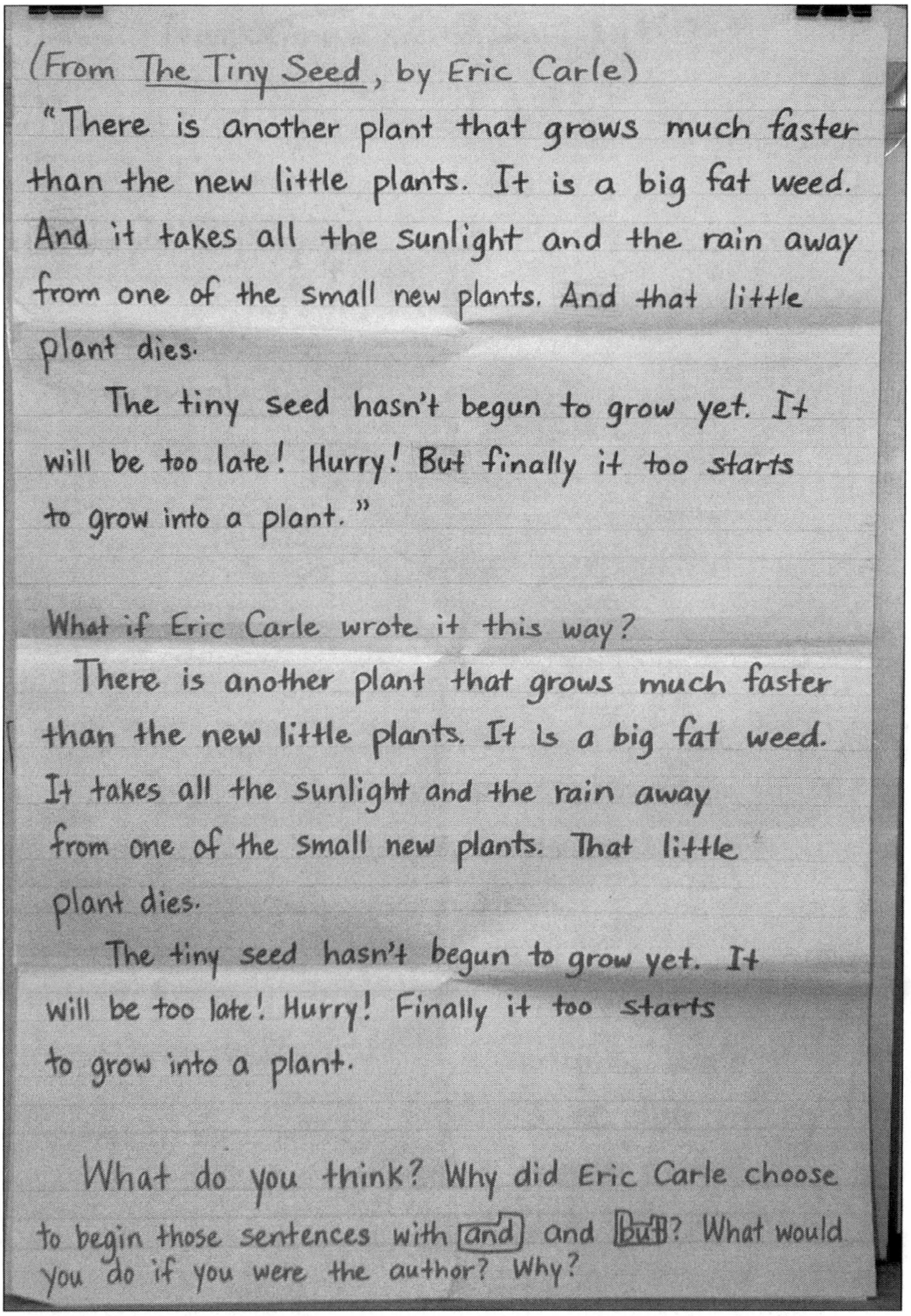

(From The Tiny Seed, by Eric Carle)

"There is another plant that grows much faster than the new little plants. It is a big fat weed. And it takes all the sunlight and the rain away from one of the small new plants. And that little plant dies.

The tiny seed hasn't begun to grow yet. It will be too late! Hurry! But finally it too starts to grow into a plant."

What if Eric Carle wrote it this way?

There is another plant that grows much faster than the new little plants. It is a big fat weed. It takes all the sunlight and the rain away from one of the small new plants. That little plant dies.

The tiny seed hasn't begun to grow yet. It will be too late! Hurry! Finally it too starts to grow into a plant.

What do you think? Why did Eric Carle choose to begin those sentences with and and but? What would you do if you were the author? Why?

Figure 3.3. Students test their hypothesis with an excerpt from *The Tiny Seed* by Eric Carle.

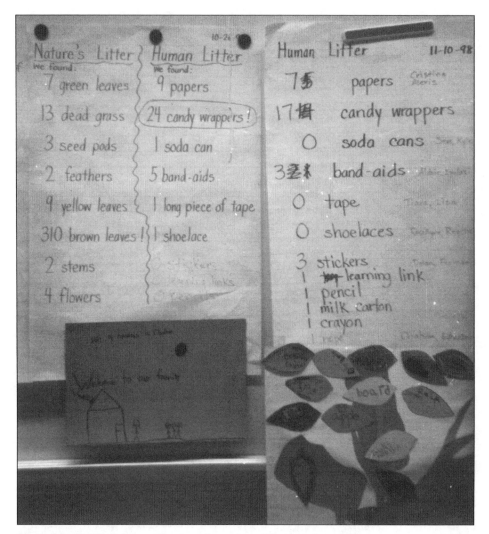

Figure 3.4. Students collect and analyze litter each month.

Over the course of this long-term investigation, every student demonstrated growth in such areas as problem solving, data analysis, and use of technology. Foremost in importance, though, was their growing awareness of their responsibility for the environment and the actions they were taking to make their world a better place.

Example 3: Producing the posters, flyers, and commercial necessitated a closer look at persuasive writing and advertising. The students realized that it wasn't so easy to create an ad or poster that would

Figure 3.5. Students share their litter data with other classes.

be noticed or believed. They studied ads that appealed to them and identified what they felt were the elements that made them effective (e.g., single focus, clear captions, eye-catching graphics), and worked to incorporate these elements into their own messages (see Figures 3.6 and 3.7). They also incorporated technology, deciding to use computers to produce the posters and flyers.

As for the commercial, they finally decided that a first-person account would be most effective. It took incredible courage for those four "razor blade boys" to appear on TV in front of the whole school and admit their wrongdoing, but they did it and they did it well.

Step 5. Possibilities

Things to consider: What possibilities, if any, do you see for extending this experience further? Go back to Step 1 and brainstorm some ideas.

Example 1: I asked the kids to continue noticing whenever they used or saw this crafting technique or whenever they helped someone else to use it, and to share what happened with the rest of us. I felt that by keeping this learning experience in the forefront of their thinking,

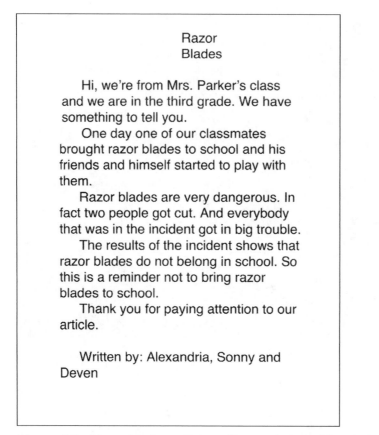

Razor
Blades

Hi, we're from Mrs. Parker's class
and we are in the third grade. We have
something to tell you.

One day one of our classmates
brought razor blades to school and his
friends and himself started to play with
them.

Razor blades are very dangerous. In
fact two people got cut. And everybody
that was in the incident got in big trouble.

The results of the incident shows that
razor blades do not belong in school. So
this is a reminder not to bring razor
blades to school.

Thank you for paying attention to our
article.

Written by: Alexandria, Sonny and
Deven

Figure 3.6. Razor Blades article written and shared by students.

there could be numerous benefits. Ray explains that for crafting techniques to be useful to writers, they must be learned "in a way that is
untied from any particular text" (127). My students would need to see
this technique in many contexts in order to generalize its application.
And, in the process, not only might they continue to use this particular
technique, but also they would perhaps begin to look much more closely
at other techniques writers used, thus deepening their understanding of
what it means to read like a writer and to craft with intention.

For many of the students, this was the most important lesson
they took from the "and-but-because" study. Beyond learning a particular crafting technique, they began to realize that writers can and do
make decisions not only about what they write, but also about how they
write, and that they choose their words with their audience in mind.

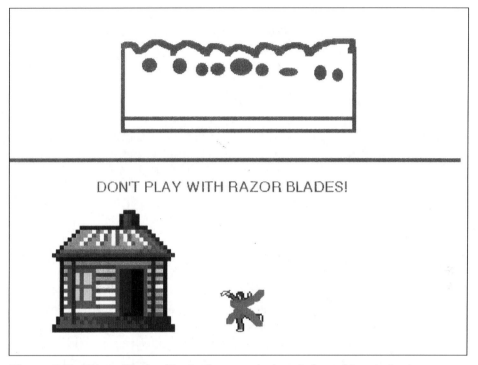

Figure 3.7. Razor Blades illustration created and shared by students (authors unknown).

Extending an experience helps us to revisit it again and again, each time building new connections and new understanding. When, through inquiry, we can help students see beyond the particular examples on their pages, we are, as Ray says, "actually teaching them a way of learning in the world that is much bigger than just learning better ways to write" (135).

Example 2: Because the class and I remained together the following year, we continued the project through second grade. Again with Gordon's help, we were able to incorporate the use of more sophisticated spreadsheet programs and, eventually, to post the project on our school website and share it with others (www.waikele.k12.hi.us/ MrsParker/LitterProject/litter_results.htm). (This project is also documented in *Teaching Children Mathematics*, the National Council of Teachers of Mathematics elementary school journal [Parker, "Take Care of Mother Earth" 414–19].)

Example 3: I suppose you could say that this learning experience was effective simply because no one else—to our knowledge, at least—ever brought razor blades to school and because the students learned more about writing. But for some of them, at least, the learning extended far beyond the study of advertising and persuasive writing to much larger social and life issues—and it happened in ways I did not expect.

Later that year, as part of a craft study of memoir writing, the kids had to write a memoir of their own choosing. One of the many memoirs we had studied was *Shortcut*, by Donald Crews. In this story, the author and his friends did something very dangerous when they were young—they took a shortcut along some railroad tracks and were almost hit by a train. Because of the connection this book had triggered for them, each of my four students decided to write his individual memoir about the razor blade incident. In part of his memoir introduction, the boy who had stolen the blades said, "I got my memoir from Donald Crews because he didn't follow any safe rules and neither did I. He even made other people involved like me because I even got my friends involved in a dangerous situation."

The level of detail they recalled, several months after the fact, was amazing. I wish you could have seen my principal's face when they read their memoirs aloud at our authors' celebration—she and I were both laughing and crying at the same time. What tickled us the most, though, was that they had used pseudonyms in their stories, as if none of us would remember that they had been the ones involved!

There's a further postscript to this incident, showing that some lessons are so powerful they keep extending themselves in ways you can never predict. Three years later, the kids studied memoir writing again, and the boy who had stolen the blades wrote again about the experience, focusing on the impression it had made on him and on how it had changed his thinking. Here are some excerpts from his sixth-grade memoir: "[This choice was] my biggest mistake. . . . When I was in third grade, I got busted for bringing razor blades to school. . . . I was dumb and I only wanted to fit in with my friends. . . . I learned that the only way to fit in is to be yourself, and not to try to be something you're not . . . if they don't like who I am, then I could make other friends instead of them."

4 Planning a Long-Term Inquiry: Our Hidden Places Project

Remember the fishing expedition I described in Chapter 2? I said that if you're lucky, one question will take you further than you ever dreamed, if you're not afraid to go with it and see where it leads you, even if you don't know ahead of time where that may be. That was the case with our Hidden Places Project. This inquiry was not necessarily one of those "save the world" events, but it resulted in rich learning and life lessons nevertheless. I share its evolution here to help you see how this long-term process played out for us and to invite you to think it through along with me and to imagine the possibilities for your own classroom.

The Hidden Places Project began with my third graders in the spring of the school year and continued through our entire fourth-grade year together. I've organized the description of this inquiry to include both my students' voices and my own, juxtaposing my students' reflections on our process with my thoughts and decision making at various points throughout. (Our project, including these student reflections, is posted on our school website: http://www.waikele.k12.hi.us/MrsParker/HiddenPlaces/waikele_hidden_places.htm. However, in this account, I've made slight changes to the order of events for clarity.)

I've also added a discussion of the many assessment opportunities embedded in this project. I end the chapter with a section for those who want to know, "Where are the standards?" I refer here to some of the ways aspects of this project connected with the curriculum standards of the National Council of Teachers of English, the International Reading Association, and the National Council of Teachers of Mathematics.

Introduction to Our Hidden Places Project

(Note: Kids' narrative, as it appears on our website, in bold.)

The Hidden Places Project started last year, in January 2001, with Dominic's broken leg. We wondered how we would help him get downstairs during a fire drill because if there was a

real fire he couldn't use the elevator. So we called the fire fight-
ers and asked how we could help him. They said we could use
the Area of Rescue Assistance.

We wondered what the Area of Rescue Assistance was for.
And then we started wondering about the Pipe Chase because
we passed it every day and we didn't know what it was.

My thoughts: What a neat opportunity for an exploration close to
home! There are so many doors I've noticed in our school that I know
nothing about—I don't know what they lead to or why they're there in
the first place. I've often wondered if the kids ever noticed or were curious about these doors. They've never said anything to me about it until
now. Have they simply not given voice to their wonderings? Or have
they not wondered about the doors at all?

I want the kids to notice things, to wonder about what they
notice, and to name and act on their wonderings. Kids love mysteries,
secret places, and adventure. Could there be possibilities here for us
to explore our school's hidden places? I'll think about this for a while.
Since we'll be together again next year, there's time to think more before
jumping in.

I wonder if we could incorporate technology in some way? What
if we took pictures of these areas and shared them with the rest of the
school as a way to extend our learning to others? Could our digital
cameras help us with this? I think I'll talk with Gordon and Ben (Gordon Wong and Ben Meyer, our technology coordinators at that time)
and ask them what they think about the possibilities. . . .

Then this year, we were reading *The Bad Beginning* by Lemony Snicket. In the story, there was a tower and the baby, Sunny,
was hanging from the tower. The book said the tower was
30 feet high and we wondered how tall our clock tower was. So
we worked on measuring our clock tower (see Figure 4.1).

My thoughts: Another question about our school building, and
what a question! Measuring the clock tower could be a great math
investigation. I definitely want to have the kids tackle that one. I wonder if there's some way it might connect with that "doors" question that
came up last spring. I'm still thinking about that question. . . .

How We Solved the Clock Tower Problem

First we brainstormed ideas about how we could measure the
clock tower. Some of the ideas were:

Put our rulers together.

Tie jump ropes or string together and hang them from the railing.

Measure the cinder blocks, count how many there are, and multiply.

We went outside to the clock tower and tried all the ideas.

When we put the rulers together, it didn't work because the clock tower was too high and we didn't have enough rulers.

When we tied the string and tried to hang it from the railing, the wind was too strong and it kept on blowing the string. Kelli Ann said maybe we should clip the name tags to the string to use them as weights, so a few people did that and then the string went to the ground. But it only measured from the bottom of the railing to the ground, 12 1/2 feet.

Some people tried measuring the cinder blocks and they got an estimate: 45 blocks times 8 inches, which equals 360 inches, or 30 feet.

But we still didn't know for sure. So then we tried measuring from the floor to the ceiling of the second floor walkway. We used Deven's measuring tape. We found out that it was 9 feet from the floor to the ceiling. We added that to the 12 1/2 feet from the string measurement and that equaled 21 1/2 feet. But we still didn't know how high the top part was, from the ceiling to the top of the clock tower.

Figure 4.1. "How will we measure the clock tower?"

Figure 4.2. Students prepare string for their balloons.

We were wondering what to try next. Then we remembered a video about Carlsbad Caverns that we watched when we were studying about caves. In the video, we saw that people who study caves sometimes have to float balloons up to the ceiling of a high cave to measure it if they can't reach it. So we decided to try floating balloons to the top of the clock tower to measure the part we couldn't reach. We planned that when the balloons touched the top we would mark the bottom of the string with tape, then pull the string down and measure it (see Figure 4.2).

We tried three times, but it was too windy (see Figure 4.3). The first balloon got stuck in a tree, the second balloon got stuck in the Hale 'Ilima building walkway, one balloon kept flopping on the roof, and the last balloon got stuck on the roof and it deflated (but we pulled it down). Oh, no!!! We were running all over the place trying to catch the balloons!

Some of us were across the courtyard at the bus shelter waiting to yell, "Stop!" when the balloons got to the top of the clock tower. They were using their rulers to see if the balloons

Figure 4.3. "Oh no!!! We were running all over the place trying to catch the balloons!"

were straight up and Sonny noticed something interesting. He asked, "How come the whole clock tower can fit inside the ruler when you're far away from it?" Mrs. Parker said that was a really interesting question and we decided to think about it some more.

My thoughts: Wow, he's talking about scale! What an opening to explore scale measurement! I need to make sure we get back to that after we've solved this immediate problem of the clock tower. I need to start checking my resources and think about how I can connect scale to something meaningful . . . hmm, could this be a way to connect the clock tower problem with the hidden places inquiry? Could the kids make scale drawings and/or scale models of the hidden places as part of the process?

We tried the balloons again on a day that wasn't too windy, but they still didn't work because there was still a little wind. Then Steven thought that maybe they worked in caves because there's no wind inside caves, but they wouldn't work outside because there's always a little wind.

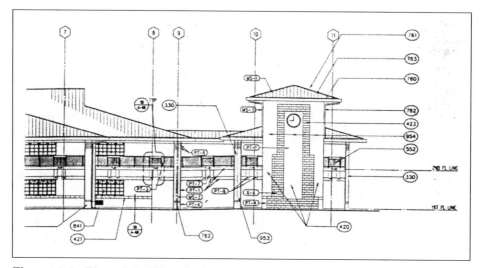

Figure 4.4. Blueprint of the clock tower.

We couldn't think of any other way to try, so we decided to look at all the information we had already and record our estimates.

My thoughts: It's time to introduce them to a resource that would help them at this point but which they wouldn't be likely to know about on their own. I'll check to see where the school blueprints are stored and to find out if we can borrow them for a while.

We wanted to know if our estimates were close, so Mrs. Parker said we could check by looking at the school blueprints. We asked Mrs. (Debora) Lum, our library media specialist, "Can we borrow the blueprints?" and she said yes.

One set of blueprints was big and one was small. We found a drawing of the clock tower in the small blueprint, and the scale on the page said 1/8" represents 1 foot (see Figure 4.4). We made a math problem out of it. Here's the problem:

"In the blueprint, the clock tower drawing is 2 inches high. If 1/8 inch represents one foot, how many feet high is the clock tower? Hint: It would be helpful to use a ruler." (Written by Steven, Keenan, Merrie-Chris, Michael, Keitaro, and Dominic.)

But when we figured out how high the clock tower would be, it came out to 16 feet, and that wasn't reasonable! We were really confused!

Then Dr. (Neil) Pateman came to visit us. He's a mathematics professor at the University of Hawai'i. We asked him, "Do you know how to read a blueprint?" and he said yes. But when he read the blueprint, he got confused, too!

We all studied the blueprints for a while, and then Dr. Pateman said, "Now I know what the problem is!"

This is what the problem was. The small blueprint was 1/4 of the size of the big blueprint, so the 1/8 inch was too small; it wasn't really 1/8 inch.

We checked the big blueprint and found another drawing of the clock tower, and that one came out right because the 1/8 inch was really 1/8 inch. Dr. Pateman explained that because they shrank the big blueprint to make the small one, that's why the small one didn't work.

So we finally found out that the clock tower is 36 feet high! It's 32 feet to the bottom of the roof and 36 feet to the top! And 32 feet was one of our estimates!

We felt so excited about solving the problem that we had a celebration!

What Happened Next

When we looked at the school blueprints to check our measurements, we saw all kinds of hidden places that we didn't know about. We were surprised! Steven said, "We barely know our own school!" We wanted to know more.

My thoughts: Okay, they're hooked and ready to be reeled in. Now they really want to know! I could tell by the questions I heard them ask as they looked at the blueprints: "What's this for?" "Why is this here?" "Wow, look at that! What is it?" It's definitely time to name those wonderings and decide what to do about them.

I think we'll start by discussing and charting what they want to know and what places they want to see. Then they'll have to develop a plan for finding out. How will they ask for permission to see those places? They'll need to contact the appropriate people . . . good opportunity to do some letter writing for an authentic purpose. . . .

We walked around the school to see what else we wanted to find out about. We made a list of the hidden places we wanted to explore and we decided to ask Mr. Bobby (Bobby Ushijima, one of our custodians) and Mr. Wong if they would give us a

October 19, 2001

Dear Dr. Matsuoka,

We are doing a project about hidden places in our school. While we were doing the clock tower problem, we noticed some places in the blueprints that we never knew about. Steven said, "We barely know about our own school," although we thought we knew before. So we decided to ask permission to take a tour around the school to learn about the places we never knew about.

Other things that made us interested were the Pipe Chase and the Area of Refuge next to our room. Every day when we pass them, we wonder what's in them or what they're for.

When we find out what's in the hidden places, we plan to make a book or put an article on our Web site so we can tell the rest of the school about it so they'll know the school better.

Mr. Wong offered to help us with the tour. He's also helping us learn how to make scale drawings so we can draw the hidden places for our book or article. And he's going to teach us how to use the digital camera so we can take pictures for the book or article.

Mr. Wong will also help us with the tour, and we're also going to ask Mr. Bobby if he will help us with the tour.

Please answer by next week Monday, October 22, so we can continue with our project. We hope you will say yes. We promise to take care of ourselves and our place and we won't touch anything we shouldn't touch.

Thank you for helping us.

Aloha,
Mrs. Parker's Class

P. S. We all wrote this together.

Figure 4.5. Class letter to Dr. Matsuoka.

tour of those places. **We wrote to Dr. Matsuoka (Diane Matsuoka, our principal) for permission to visit the hidden places** (see Figure 4.5).

We wrote to Mr. Bobby and Mr. Greg (Greg DeSamito, another of our custodians), Mr. Wong and Mr. Meyer, to ask them if they'd take us on a tour of the hidden places.

My thoughts: We'll need to do some preparation up front, making sure the kids are able to take care of themselves, each other, and our place when we go on the tour. Whole-class discussions are in order here. And I'll need to make sure the kids follow up with appropriate thank-you notes.

Also, note-taking is going to be really important when we go on the tour: How will they decide what's important or interesting enough to jot down? What's their purpose for taking notes at all? What will they do with the information they're gathering? We need to have some conversations about this. . . .

We took the tour with Mr. Bobby and Mr. Wong (see Figure 4.6). **We took notes on the tour so we'd remember the information we were learning. We wrote thank-you notes to Mr. Bobby and Mr. Wong for taking us on the tour.**

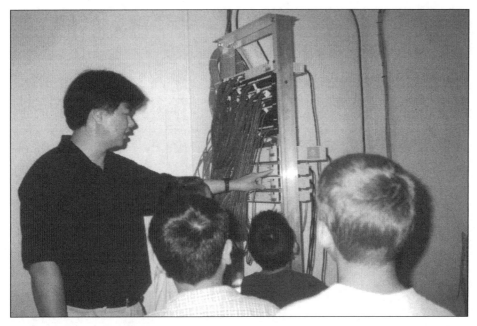

Figure 4.6. Gordon Wong shows students the computer network cables in the Intermediate Distribution Frame, one of the hidden places in the school.

The tour was fun because we got to see places we never saw before. Even Mrs. Parker (our teacher) never saw some of those places before! We found out that everything in our school is here for a reason. There are all kinds of things that make our school work better.

My thoughts: We all learned a lot on the tour. We need to discuss it again as a whole class. Now that we have this information, what actions, if any, will we take? Is this information worth sharing? Would others want or need to know about our school's hidden places? How could it benefit others if we shared this information?

We thought it would be fair to share our learning so that other people will know more about our school because we're all a learning 'ohana (family).

My thoughts: How might we share our learning? The kids could sketch what they've seen, but I still wonder if photos might be better for this purpose. What about the digital camera? It would certainly enhance the quality and clarity of what they'd be sharing. Here's a perfect opportunity to connect them to another resource that can help them. Back to Gordon and Ben to see if they'll provide the instruction.

We learned how to use the digital camera so we could take pictures of the hidden places (Mr. Wong and Mr. Meyer taught all of us how to use the camera).

My thoughts: They know what they want to do and why they want to do it, and they now have the tools to do it as well. Now, how are we going to organize for the work of carrying out this project? It's kind of a big project, after all. I think the kids need to do the thinking and problem solving here. Also, by deciding on the organization themselves, they'll understand and own the process. We can always evaluate and make adjustments together as we go along.

We decided on groups for reporting (four table groups) and decided which group would report on which buildings.

My thoughts: I'll have the kids work out the small-group schedules with Gordon and Ben. Then they'll be responsible for being prepared when it's their group's turn.

Each group went back with Mr. Wong and Mr. Meyer to take the pictures of the hidden places in their buildings.

My thoughts: Now that they have taken their pictures, they'll have to decide which pictures they want to use and how they want to describe and explain each one to make it interesting and understandable to their intended audience.

Now's the time for us to start revisiting the charts we made when we studied nonfiction writing last year in third grade (see Figure 4.7). I think we'll spend a few days looking back at the craft techniques we noticed and documented so the kids can start thinking about how they want to craft their writing about this project.

Each group chose the pictures they wanted to use and wrote captions for them (see Figure 4.8). **We all helped each other revise and edit our captions. Some people had to go back and get more information and pictures.**

My thoughts: When the kids realized as they edited their captions that they didn't have all the information they needed, this provided a great opening to link back to our nonfiction study from the point of view of both reader and writer: How do we feel as readers if we read nonfiction text that's unclear or inaccurate? How do we even know if what we read is accurate? What's our obligation as writers to make sure that what we write is as accurate as we can possibly make it?

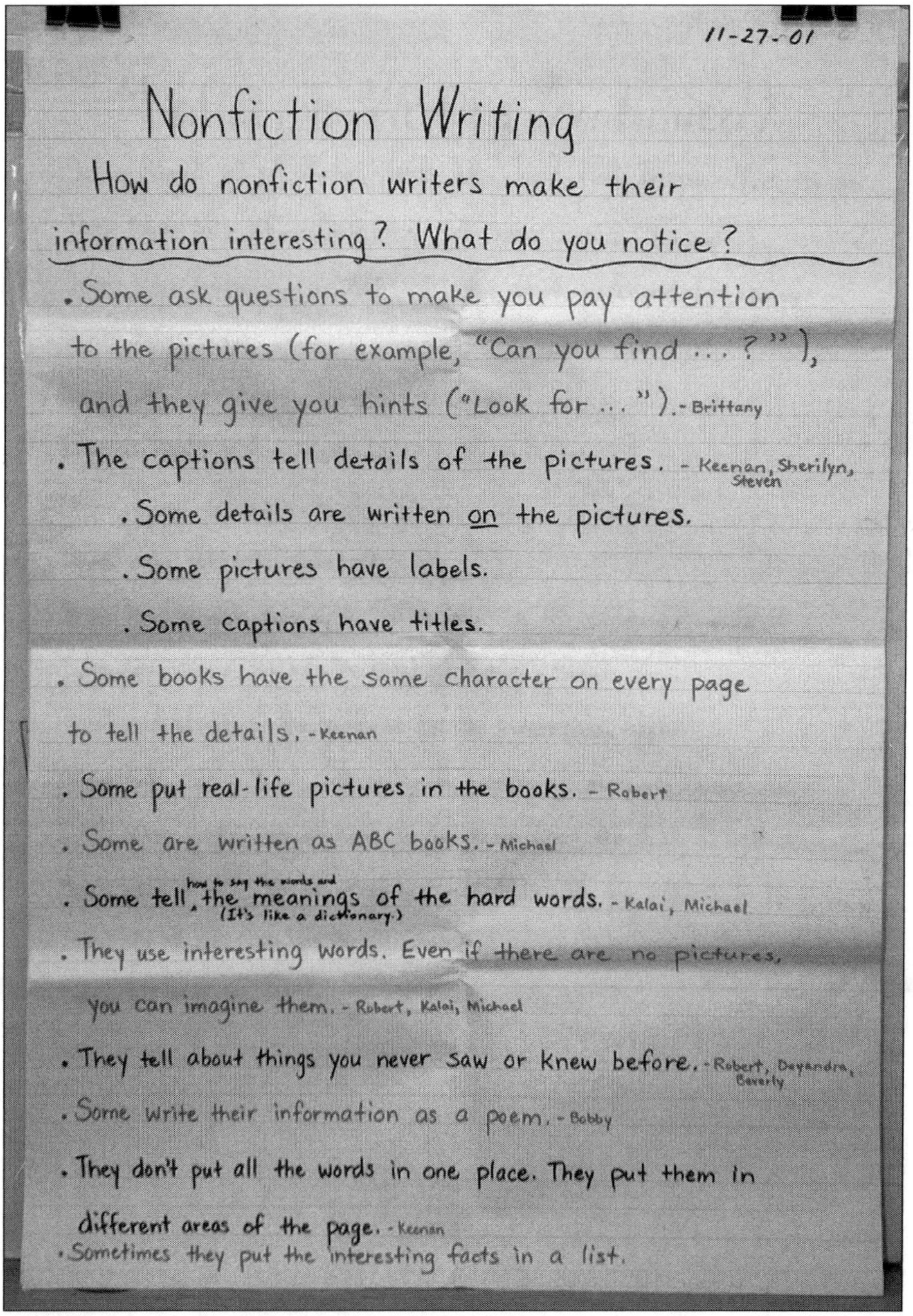

11-27-01

Nonfiction Writing

How do nonfiction writers make their information interesting? What do you notice?

- Some ask questions to make you pay attention to the pictures (for example, "Can you find ... ?"), and they give you hints ("Look for ..."). - Brittany
- The captions tell details of the pictures. - Keenan, Sherilyn, Steven
  - Some details are written <u>on</u> the pictures.
  - Some pictures have labels.
  - Some captions have titles.
- Some books have the same character on every page to tell the details. - Keenan
- Some put real-life pictures in the books. - Robert
- Some are written as ABC books. - Michael
- Some tell how to say the words and the meanings of the hard words. (It's like a dictionary.) - Kalai, Michael
- They use interesting words. Even if there are no pictures, you can imagine them. - Robert, Kalai, Michael
- They tell about things you never saw or knew before. - Robert, Deyandra, Beverly
- Some write their information as a poem. - Bobby
- They don't put all the words in one place. They put them in different areas of the page. - Keenan
- Sometimes they put the interesting facts in a list.

Figure 4.7. Charts from third-grade study of nonfiction writing craft techniques.

Continued

Figure 4.7 continued

Nonfiction Writing (continued)   12-4-01

- Some show what places look like and how people live. —Kawika
- They have lots of information on one topic. —Dominic
- Some give addresses or Web sites for more information. —Sonny
- Some have maps. —Sonny
- Some are like guides. —Tracy, Kawika, Sonny
- They tell about things people would want to know.
- Some have pop-up pictures. —Jadine, Robert
- Some have fold-out pictures.
- Some have arrows pointing to the captions and/or pictures. —Keenan
- Some have speech balloons to catch your eye. —Sherilyn
- Some are wordless. The pictures get you interested. —Irvin
- Some have funny, scary, interesting, or surprising pictures. —Aldrich
- Some have useful introductions so you know what the book is about. —Keenan
- Some have a make-believe story and real facts (like the Magic School Bus). —Tracy
- Some have diagrams so you can see inside things (buildings, bodies, etc.). —Devan, Kaitara
- Some tell about the old days or the future. —Bobby, Aldrich, Kawika, Sonny

Figure 4.8. Students helped each other revise and edit their caption drafts.

> **We resized our pictures and inserted them into our text files. (Mr. Wong and Mr. Meyer taught all of us how to do that.)**

My thoughts: The photos and captions are finally complete. Now for the connection back to the scale drawings in the blueprints. It's coming together after all!

More Connections

> **When we looked in the blueprints we learned about scale drawings and how to read them. (Sonny's question about the clock tower and his ruler helped us think about scale drawings.)**

My thoughts: They've gotten pretty good at reading the scale drawings in the blueprints. Now I really want to follow this idea and

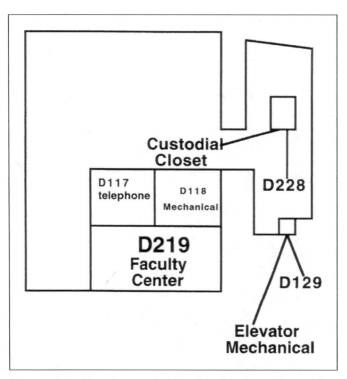

Figure 4.9. Practice scale drawing (author unknown).

link it to the Hidden Places Project, maybe even incorporating more technology. I think I'll talk with Gordon and Neil to find out if they know of any age-appropriate software for creating scale drawings. The accuracy the kids could obtain with the computer might help them understand the concept of scale even better. I need to find out soon because I want to explore it and decide for myself if it would fit.

> **We learned how to make scale drawings and practiced drawing classroom things** (see Figure 4.9). **First we sketched our drawings and then we did them on the computer. (Mrs. Parker taught us how to do scale drawings and Mr. Wong taught us how to do them on the computer.)**

My thoughts: The next organizational piece is a big one. We'll facilitate but they have to see the big picture. It will take time, but that's okay. No matter how long it takes or how messy the process, the kids need to be the ones to make these decisions if they're going to learn the most from the experience.

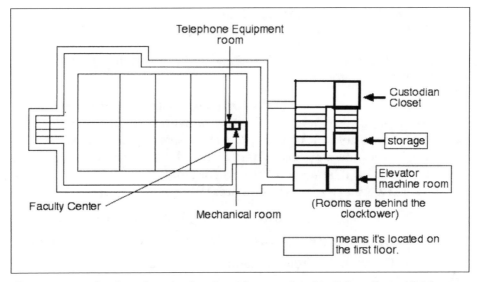

Figure 4.10. Students' scale drawing of one school building (from Hidden Places Project website).

We worked with Mr. Wong, Mr. Meyer, and Mrs. Parker to decide how to organize our project. Mr. Wong said it was like a giant puzzle and we were each making the pieces and then we would put all the pieces together. We thought for a long time about how we wanted to do that. We talked about it a lot.

We decided it would be neat to organize our project by buildings and we decided to start each section with a scale drawing of the building. We made our scale drawings of the buildings (see Figure 4.10). We used the blueprints to help us.

My thoughts: Yes, it's really coming together!

We thought about other things to help us organize our project and make it interesting to our audience. We remembered that sometimes in the nonfiction books we study they have a little character who guides you through the book, so we decided to have a talking clock tower as our guide. We thought that would make sense because the clock tower is a symbol of our school and it kind of started the whole project.

My thoughts: Revisiting those nonfiction charts is paying off. I need to keep that connection in the forefront for them as they move closer toward publication.

We did a blind review of our talking clock tower drawings and picked the one we wanted to use.

My thoughts: They're almost ready to publish. It's time to take a look at possibilities together.

We brainstormed ideas for ways to share our project with the rest of our school. The ideas were: newsletter; posters; Internet; book; KWAI 97 (student news); and sharing in person. We made a criteria chart to decide what might work best. We decided to share on the Internet and make a book, because those two ways met all our criteria:

1. **Has to be interesting, exciting, and show our feelings.**
2. **Has to help our audience understand what we learned.**
3. **Has to help them remember what we learned.**
4. **They should be able to go back to the information.**
5. **The information should be available to everybody.**
6. **We need to be able to fit all our information in.**

We decided that we'd use the other ideas (newsletter, posters, KWAI 97 News [our school closed-circuit television news program], and sharing in person) to advertise our project and get people interested in it.

My thoughts: The project has gotten so big (i.e., there's such a huge collection of pages) that the kids might need some help with organizing it so they won't lose sight of the whole. But again, they'll really have to do the organizing themselves in order to understand it. I'll have them work in groups, with each group making its own organizational chart, and then we can look at everything all together (see Figure 4.11). After that they'll be ready to start putting their project up on the Internet with Gordon's and Ben's help.

We made giant flowcharts to organize what would go first, next, etc.

Each group worked with Mr. Wong and Mr. Meyer to put a draft of our whole project on the Internet. Mr. Wong made us a secret spot on our school website to hide our draft so we could check it. We were the only ones who knew about it!

We worked as a whole class to revise and edit our draft. We checked everything all together. We checked several times.

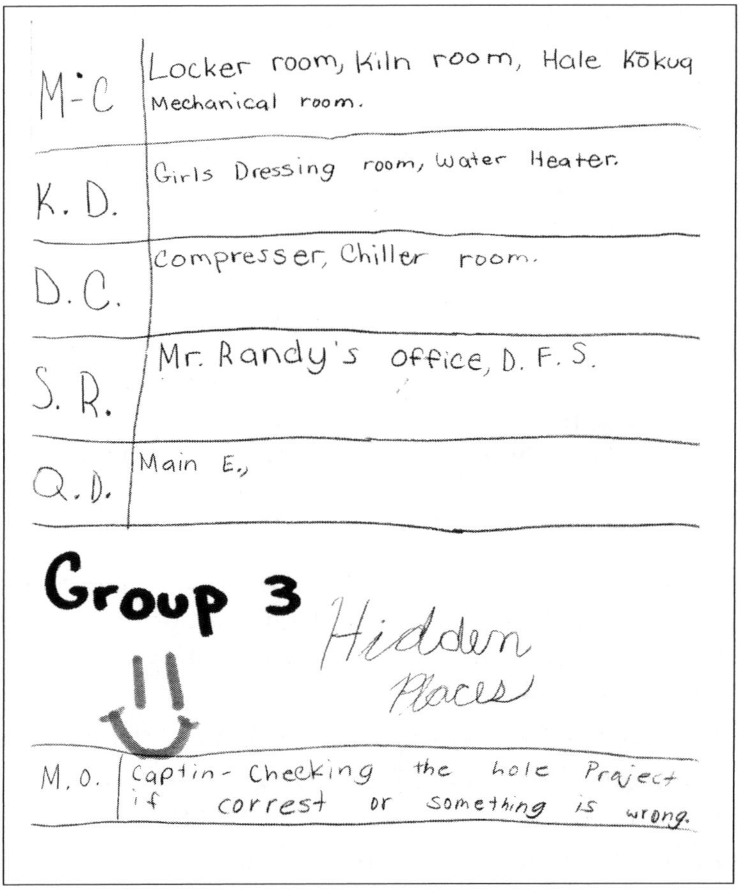

Figure 4.11. One group's organizational chart (author unknown).

My thoughts: They're so into their revising and editing. . . . I don't think I've ever seen them spend as much time deliberating over so many drafts. This definitely shows what kids will put their hearts into when there's a real sense of purpose and audience attached to their work.

Now there's still the group that wants to do the video; . . . here's a chance to incorporate yet another aspect of technology.

> **Mr. Meyer worked with Merrie-Chris, Tracy Ann, and Sherilyn to make a short video to advertise our project on the KWAI News.**
>
> **This was a BIG research project! It took a LONG time, more than six months, but we think it was worth it! We hope you'll**

think so, too. We've been working on this project for a long time because we think it's important and we've been learning a lot by doing it.

We think our school is designed better than some other schools because it helps us with our learning. We appreciate our school even more now that we learned more about it.

What's Next?

But that wasn't the end of our project; it couldn't be, because authentic inquiries can't help but lead to others. Here's what the kids said:

> Our Hidden Places Project isn't finished because it gave us lots of ideas about other things we want to know about. We think it might never be finished! Here are some of the things we're doing and thinking of doing next:
>
> 1. When we started the Hidden Places Project, we had a lot of questions. But when we started getting the answers to some of our questions, we had MORE questions! Here are some of our questions:
>
>   - How much money did it cost to build the whole school?
>   - . . . plus the playground, jump ropes, balls, and other things we play and learn about? (Sherilyn)
>   - Who has the main key besides Mr. Bobby?
>   - I want to learn more about the underground places. (Keitaro)
>   - If there was lots of stuff and little room, what would they do to put away the stuff? (Irvin)
>   - Why is the pipe chase so skinny? Who made it that way?
>   - Who made the stairs to the attic so steep?
>   - How big is the attic?
>   - Who thought of making a room in a room in a room? (Kelli Ann)
>   - What if the key is missing? Does someone have another one like that at home? (Aldrich)
>   - Why is there a gym in the attic?
>   - Why is the pipe chase room so small? (Tracy Ann)

- Why is there a false ceiling? (Deven)
- Why do they have a gym in the penthouse? (Merrie-Chris)
- How much did this school cost altogether? (Kawika)
- Will they build more buildings for the school so just in case more kids come we'll have enough space?
- Why didn't you tell us about these hidden places we never knew about before? (Robert)
- What's above the penthouse?
- Why were the area of refuge and the pipe chase cold inside? (Keenan)
- How much does everything in the school cost together?
- How come the pipe chase is so skinny?
- How come there's a fake ceiling? (Sonny)
- Why did they make the workout place and Hale Kokua? (Dominic)
- How do the machines work?
- How much do the machines cost? (Steven)
- I want to learn more about the penthouse.
- How can people fit in the pipe chase?
- Why did you put all these hidden places in the school? (Deyandra)
- How much did one classroom cost?
- How long is the office?
- How long are the pipes? (Bobby)
- Why didn't they tell us that the ceiling was fake for all these years? (Brittany)
- Why do the ceiling parts come out? Why is it like that? (Beverly)
- Why did they put a gym in the attic?
- How did they plan the school?
- What made them put hidden places in the school? Why did they have a feeling to put hidden places in the school? (Sunshine)

We're going to try to find the answers to some of these questions. We think it will be interesting. We also think we'll probably have even MORE questions!

2. We're going to try to make scale models from the scale drawings we made of all the buildings in our school. If we like the way the models turn out, we're going to use them to help advertise our project.

3. We've been designing our own creative houses with hidden places. Some of us might make scale models of these houses.

4. Some of us have been thinking about writing our own "hidden places" mystery stories. We think it would be neat to write a story about the Mechanical Equipment Penthouse or some other hidden place in our school!

5. Some people in our class want to become architects and engineers when they grow up. They're trying to learn more about these jobs.

We'll probably have more ideas later. What ideas do you have? Let us know!

Life Lessons

And here's what they said they learned from the experience:

Here are some of the life lessons we've learned from doing this project:

SHARE YOUR LEARNING . . .
It helps others learn, too.

SHARE ACCURATE INFORMATION . . .
So others will learn and ask questions.

KEEP ASKING QUESTIONS . . .
So you can learn more!

What about Assessment?

Authentic, classroom-based assessment should be inseparable and virtually indistinguishable from curriculum and instruction. Assessment of our hidden places inquiry involved process as well as products, and it played an important role throughout.

Because this was a yearlong, multidisciplinary inquiry project rather than a single, isolated event, the Hidden Places Project addressed standards across content areas, both simultaneously and over time; and it allowed me to assess my students' performance in a variety of authentic contexts.

One way I assess my students is through anecdotal records based on direct observation of their performance on a variety of tasks. In mathematics, for example, I observed them in the process of solving the clock tower problem. I listened to their reasoning as we discussed various issues and procedures. I could see who was able to think through the problem successfully, who needed help, and who contributed ideas and seemed to understand as we tested and analyzed theories and worked toward a solution. I could see who was able to offer and recognize reasonable estimates and apply basic computational and measurement skills, who noticed and understood when the results of their measurements (as with the blueprint dilemma) were not reasonable, and who offered suggestions for new ways to approach the problem when things didn't go as planned. In a similar fashion, I observed their thinking processes and performance with regard to understanding scale, creating scale models, and reading and interpreting blueprints.

While I continually observe my students' work in process, I also evaluate their finished products. Many such products were generated during this inquiry: the clock tower problem pages; a variety of scale drawings, done both by hand and on the computer; notes from our tour of the hidden places; letters to school personnel; and photo captions and other informational writing as the project was developed, advertised, and posted on our website.

In our previous study of nonfiction writing, students had read and explored various types of nonfiction literature, discussed and recorded what they noticed, and eventually defined and set criteria for writing informational text. They had studied how authors craft their nonfiction writing through a series of lessons I had developed in response to their observations and wonderings. Some of the topics for these craft lessons had included ways to make information interesting and understandable; ways to help readers ask their own questions; use of pictures, diagrams, and labels; and possible organizational formats.

The student work resulting from this inquiry could be assessed according to many overlapping standards. I used our state writing assessment and language arts standards and the student-developed criteria for writing informational text as my guides. I looked for clarity and purpose: how the writing conveyed meaning, provided important and accurate information, showed knowledge of the subject, and was appropriate for its intended audience.

Student self-assessment was also an integral part of the process throughout this inquiry. Students must learn how to evaluate their own work if they are to become responsible for their learning. Students individually self-assessed their problem-solving strategies and informational writing according to the classroom criteria we had developed. Through ongoing reflective discussions, I also encouraged the students to continually assess our progress as a whole class: where we were at each step along the way; what was working and not working so far; what new questions we had at that point; and what our next steps should be. This kept the focus on our collective purpose while reaffirming each individual's responsibility toward achieving our goal.

These examples cover only some aspects of the mathematics and writing involved in this inquiry. Yet there was so much more to it than that, crossing content-area boundaries and encompassing social matters as well. You will probably find other connections as you look back at this chapter. Could any single test have captured the depth of an inquiry such as this one? Any such instrument that would seek to reduce learning to a number would, in my view at least, do a terrible disservice to both learning and learners; authentic inquiries demand authentic assessments.

Where Are the Standards?

As ideally envisioned, standards should be guides but not prescriptions. As ideally implemented, they cannot be separated from each other. Just as inquiry transcends arbitrary subject-area boundaries, "ideal" standards overlap each other, encompass broad understandings, and emerge naturally from rich learning experiences.

Mathematics Standards

Let's look first at how the Hidden Places Project addressed the National Council of Teachers of Mathematics standards for grades 3 through 5. Here are a few examples of what my students needed to know and be able to do, in varying degrees, as they measured the clock tower, learned about and created their scale drawings, used technology, and shared their learning with others.

> Number and Operations Standard: Understand numbers, ways of representing numbers, relationships among numbers, and number systems; Compute fluently and make reasonable estimates.

Geometry Standard: Use visualization, spatial reasoning, and geometric modeling to solve problems.

Measurement Standard: Understand measurable attributes of objects and the units, systems, and processes of measurement; Apply appropriate techniques, tools, and formulas to determine measurements.

Problem Solving Standard: Build new mathematical knowledge through problem solving; Apply and adapt a variety of appropriate strategies to solve problems; Monitor and reflect on the process of mathematical problem solving.

Communication Standard: Communicate their mathematical thinking coherently and clearly to peers, teachers, and others.

Connections Standard: Recognize and apply mathematics in contexts outside of mathematics.

Representation Standard: Create and use representations to organize, record, and communicate mathematical ideas; Use representations to model and interpret physical, social, and mathematical phenomena. (*Principles and Standards* 148–206)

Language Arts Standards

The National Council of Teachers of English/International Reading Association *Standards for the English Language Arts* work in the same way to incorporate the various interrelated aspects of literacy. Here are some of the things my students needed to know and be able to do, again in varying degrees, as they wrote letters, took notes on the tour, wrote and revised their captions based on their in-depth study of nonfiction writing, and organized, published, and advertised their work.

Standard 1: Students read a wide range of print and nonprint texts to build an understanding of texts, of themselves, and of the cultures of the United States and the world; to acquire new information; to respond to the needs and demands of society and the workplace; and for personal fulfilment. Among these texts are fiction and nonfiction, classic and contemporary works. . . .

Standard 4: Students adjust their use of spoken, written, and visual language (e.g., conventions, style, vocabulary) to communicate effectively with a variety of audiences and for different purposes.

Standard 5: Students employ a wide range of strategies as they write and use different writing process elements appropriately to communicate with different audiences for a variety of purposes.

Standard 6: Students apply knowledge of language structure, language conventions (e.g., spelling and punctuation), media techniques, figurative language, and genre to create, critique, and discuss print and nonprint texts.

Standard 7: Students conduct research on issues and interests by generating ideas and questions, and by posing problems. They gather, evaluate, and synthesize data from a variety of sources (e.g., print and nonprint texts, artifacts, people) to communicate their discoveries in ways that suit their purpose and audience. . . .

Standard 11: Students participate as knowledgeable, reflective, creative, and critical members of a variety of literacy communities.

Standard 12: Students use spoken, written, and visual language to accomplish their own purposes (e.g., for learning, enjoyment, persuasion, and the exchange of information). (25)

These are a few of the standards that this project addressed. If you look at the NCTE/IRA and NCTM standards documents and perhaps those of other national curricular organizations, as well as your own state or local standards, you'll probably see further connections. You might want to take a few minutes to jot down some of those connections for yourself and to think about the difference between "starting with the standards" and guiding their emergence throughout the process. Would it have been possible to envision, pre-plan, or carry out this project simply by looking at a list of standards and creating some lessons beforehand?

Thinking about the Possibilities

I hope this more or less step-by-step account has helped to show a bit about my decision making, as well as my students' thoughts, throughout this project. It's important to remember that this same question—What are the hidden places in our school?—could have gone in totally different directions, and that's okay. There's no one right or wrong way. And there's nothing inherently magical about this particular question. I certainly don't expect anyone to replicate this project; that wasn't my intent in sharing the project in such detail. But I hope it will help you understand a little more about how the responsive/reflective lesson planning process works and that you'll give it a try. Whatever happens in your classroom depends on you, your kids, and the resources, including people and technology, available to you. But with kids' curiosity driving the process, you as the teacher just need to think about how to guide it and milk it for all it's worth. What possibilities do you see right now, for yourself and your class?

5 Teaching for Inquiry

Throughout this book, I've talked a lot about the importance of listening to children's questions as we plan for inquiry. But it's the questions we ask our students, and the way we guide discussions and learning engagements in response to their questions, that are the keys to fostering inquiry. What happens in the classroom—whether inquiry is truly inquiry—depends upon the discourse that is established there.

The term *discourse* refers to "the ways in which knowledge is constructed and exchanged in classrooms. . . . [T]eachers play a crucial role in shaping the discourse of their classrooms through the signals they send about the knowledge and ways of thinking and knowing that are valued" (Ball 44).

Discourse encompasses both verbal and nonverbal aspects of the learning environment. In this chapter, however, I'll focus on talk. Classroom talk involves fundamental social issues: how ideas are exchanged, who talks, how the talk flows, and how the teacher facilitates that talk. The classroom is a place of social interaction. The teacher's role is to guide and shape that interaction in order to support student learning and to encourage all students to take an active role in that learning. This type of dialogue is not always easy to envision or carry out, because many of us experienced the opposite in our own schooling: Teacher asks the questions, students answer, teacher says if answer is correct or not—period.

One study on teacher questioning found that "teachers commonly ask as many as fifty thousand questions a year and their students as few as ten questions each. Further, about 80 percent of teacher questions are likely to call for memory processes only" (Watson and Young 126). Other researchers have found similar patterns of questioning occurring from the earliest grades through high school.

To create a more thoughtful classroom, we need to move toward different patterns of dialogue and teacher questioning, those which can guide our students beyond recall of facts and toward deeper thinking (see Figure 5.1). But how do we do this? How can we create a community of learners who think together and share ideas? Several years ago, I asked myself those same questions, and my search for the answers ultimately changed my teaching. In this chapter, I'd like to share some of the things I found out that have helped me the most. I'll discuss

Facilitating Discussions That Promote Inquiry

Turn the Thinking Back to the Students

- What do you think?
- How could you find out?
- How could you solve this problem?
- What ideas do you have?
- What could you try next?

Focus on Students' Thinking

- What made you think of that?
- Can you explain your reasoning?
- How did you solve that problem?
- What made you decide to try that strategy?
- How would you explain that idea to others?

Probe to Clarify and Explore Students' Thinking and Promote Reflection

- Tell me more about ___.
- What did you do first? Next?
- What made you decide to solve the problem that way?
- Where did you get stuck and what did you do when that happened?
- What did you wonder about when you were working on ___?
- What pictures are you seeing in your mind to help you think about that?

Redirect Students to Each Other

- Did you hear what ___ said?
- Could you repeat what you said so everyone can hear it?
- What do you think about that idea?
- Do you agree or disagree? Why?
- What would you like to add to what ___ said?

Treat Even Routine Procedures and Social Issues Reflectively

- What happened? What do you think caused that to happen?
- How do you think ___ felt when that happened?
- How would you feel if that happened to you?
- What could you have done instead?
- How could we help ___ so that won't happen again?

Figure 5.1. Facilitating discussions that promote inquiry.

some general principles and specific strategies for facilitating the type of classroom discourse that can encourage and guide inquiry.

Different Types of Questions

First, let's consider why we'd want to ask questions of our students in the first place. If we want to promote inquiry, there are four reasons for doing so:

- To encourage learners to think for themselves
- To explore their thinking
- To facilitate their understanding
- To encourage higher-level thinking

To accomplish these goals, we need to be aware of the difference between asking questions that seek recall of facts and asking those that look deeper. Jean Piaget categorized question types into four categories that progress from lower- to higher-order thinking:

- Direct Information Questions: These ask for information that is already known or readily available (e.g., What was the name of the girl in the story? How much is two plus two?).

- Focusing Questions: These guide in a certain focused direction, asking the learner to compare, analyze, explain, and so forth, but the child constructs his/her own response (e.g., How were these two stories alike or different? What patterns do you see in this number chart?).

- Valuing Questions: These ask children to make judgments (e.g., Which character did you like best, and why? Why did you decide to solve this problem in that way?).

- Open-Ended Questions: These ask children to think more broadly and to reach for more possibilities, interpretations, or solutions (e.g., In what other ways might this story character solve his problem? In how many ways can you make the number ten?). (Labinowicz 227)

I've listed these question types here not to imply that only one kind should be used (there's a time and place for all) or that they should be asked in any particular order, but because I found their categorizations helpful as I began to recognize them and thus to use them more consciously and flexibly. Piaget, of course, is certainly not the only person who has categorized questions according to a thought hierarchy. Other researchers have done the same thing in similar ways that would be equally helpful to think about. The main thing is that we recognize that different questions ask for different kinds of thinking, so that we can reflect on our own ways of questioning our students.

So, keeping in mind our reasons for asking questions and the different types of questions we might ask, here are some general principles for facilitating classroom discussions that stand to promote inquiry.

Turn the Thinking Back to the Students

I've learned over the years, sometimes the hard way, that whenever possible, I need to throw the kids' questions right back at them—that they are the ones who need to do the thinking. You'll see instances of this in the examples of the framework in use (Chapter 3) and the Hidden Places Project (Chapter 4). When my first graders asked, "How can you measure something that's longer than a ruler if you only have one ruler?" I could have just told them immediately about other, more efficient means of measuring longer lengths. But their explorations helped them develop a deeper conceptual understanding of linear measurement, so that when I did introduce them later to measuring tapes and other standard tools for measuring, they were able to understand better why these instruments were developed and how they are used.

It was the same with the clock tower problem. In trying to measure the clock tower themselves, the kids had to develop and test a number of theories. When those theories didn't work, they had to rethink their hypotheses and develop new theories. They did exactly what mathematicians do; they became mathematicians. I could have told them about the blueprints right away, but think of all that would have been lost if I hadn't waited until I felt the time was right. You can see from their reflections how much they enjoyed the challenge and the satisfaction they derived from finally solving the problem.

I need to say a few things here about learning and "hard" problems. Many people say that learning should be "fun," and I had always agreed. But my definition of "fun" in relation to learning changed as I observed my students over the years. I began to notice that the problems they considered to be the most fun seemed to be the most demanding. And as I reflected on this paradox, I realized that the "fun" came from the intellectual challenge involved in successfully solving meaningful problems. That's why the kids celebrated so joyfully after solving the clock tower problem. They felt a true sense of accomplishment, and they felt ready to tackle more "hard" problems.

This is how we want our students to feel. It's that frustration-persistence-satisfaction cycle, in an atmosphere that encourages and supports their efforts, that drives their learning and keeps their curiosity alive. It's crucial to try to guide students toward learning engagements that are challenging but not totally beyond them, and this is why our curricular decisions have to be based on our deep knowledge of learners, learning, and content.

I can't say enough about the importance of this first principle. If you can develop in yourself the habit of turning the thinking back to the students, you will have taken one of the greatest steps toward fostering inquiry. And don't give up if this doesn't seem to work right away; it probably won't at first. With every new class, I have students looking at me blankly or saying, "It's too hard! Just tell us!" even holding their heads as if thinking were just too painful. If yours do the same, stand firm, show that you're confident they can do it, and accept the ideas they do come up with, even if their initial attempts don't reflect the kind of thinking you're hoping for. You can build from there. Your goal at this point is to establish the understanding that they are capable of thinking and that you won't do it for them—and that you are truly interested in what they are thinking.

One more point: Don't worry if a problem isn't solved within one class period. It's okay to let it hang there for a while and to keep coming back to it, even several days or weeks later, or longer, as with our Hidden Places Project, if the interest is still there. Just say something like, "Let's think some more and we'll talk about it again tomorrow." This was one of the most difficult things for me to learn. As teachers, we often feel the need for "closure" with every lesson. But rich, complex problems and issues can't always be neatly wrapped up like thirty-minute television shows, and some can't be solved at all. Many people believe that kids who are accustomed to thinking about and reflecting on questions over time will be less likely to become frustrated and give up when they're facing difficult tasks, whether in school or in life. Often, too, reflecting on and revisiting a problem can help the kids accomplish things that you—and they—might have thought were beyond them. Turning the thinking back to them, and then giving them the time to think, can have a powerful influence on teaching and learning.

Here are some examples of questions you can ask to turn the thinking back to the students:

- What do you think?
- How could you find out?
- How could you solve this problem?
- What ideas do you have?
- What could you try next?

Be sure to chart the ideas students offer in response to your questions, crediting them on the chart for each idea they contribute. They love this validation; it tells them that their thinking is indeed important, and that thinking is expected and valued in their classroom.

Focus on Students' Thinking

Because I study children's thinking closely, I often take notes during class discussions. When the kids first see me doing this and ask me about it, I tell them, "I'm writing down what you say because I'm interested in what you're thinking and how you're learning; it helps me learn more about how to teach." They get so used to my doing this that they'll remind me if I've become so engrossed in a discussion that I forget to write down what's being said! (I also use a microcassette recorder at times, but I still like to jot down notes for myself in case the recorder doesn't pick up some of the kids' comments.)

It's critical to focus on students' thinking, not on "right" answers, and to listen carefully to what they say. If we look again at the example of the clock tower problem, we can see that some of the suggestions that were made for solving it were obviously not going to work. But again, the suggestions were evidence that the kids were thinking, and it was important to honor and record all of them. It's not up to me, as the teacher, to place a value judgment on each idea; that's something for the kids to figure out as they go along. It's more important to list every idea offered so the students won't be afraid to share for fear of being "wrong." Once all the ideas are listed, that chart becomes a permanent record to which the class can refer again and again, and upon which they can reflect as they bring new experiences and understanding to their study.

Be careful to avoid expressing your opinion about the ideas shared. Try to refrain from giving judgmental feedback, such as "Very good!" or "Great job!" There are several problems with this type of verbal praise. First, it's based on the assumption that adults are the sole authorities who can pass judgment on their students' efforts. It limits learners' self-reflection, and thereby their development as autonomous thinkers. Students begin to feel that they'll only be praised for responses that mirror what the teacher is looking for, so if they don't think they can guess what's on the teacher's mind, they won't respond at all. Discussions become much more narrow, with contributions coming only from those students who feel "safe"—often for the wrong reasons.

Another problem with verbal praise is that it sets kids up against each other, making the formation of a true learning community much more difficult. If we say, "Great answer!" to one student, others in the class might then decide that the answers they were thinking of would probably not be great, so again, they'll not respond at all. Plus, they're probably not feeling very kindly toward the student who gave the "great" answer, because he or she got all the praise and they didn't.

We can help kids to know that we value what they think, and to empower them as independent learners, by responding to their process rather than to their answers. When you ask the kids, "How did you figure that out?" it lets them know that you appreciate their thinking but it pushes them to think further at the same time. Similar kinds of responses can help them feel valued while helping them extend their thinking process (e.g., "I wonder if that would happen if you tried it again?"; "What are some other ways you might solve this problem?"; and see other sample questions below).

Another useful technique is to offer acceptance in a non-direct way. Instead of making direct comments about a student's answer, we can ask the class, "What other ideas do you have?" Such a response implies our acceptance of the first student's idea, but offers a way to extend the discussion to all.

If we focus only on answers, whether right or wrong, we miss opportunities for valuable insights into our students' thinking. A good rule of thumb is to take a "How do you know?" rather than a "Who knows?" approach when we respond to kids' ideas (Schwartz 399), and to ask them questions that are designed to help them reflect on and extend their thinking. This is praise of a much more genuine nature.

Here are some examples of questions you can ask to focus on the students' thinking:

- What made you think of that?
- Can you explain your reasoning?
- How did you solve that problem?
- What made you decide to try that strategy?
- How would you explain that idea to others?

Probe to Clarify and Explore Students' Thinking and Promote Reflection

This is another very important principle. If we want deep thinking, we need to dig for it. Unless a question is one that requires only brief, factual information (e.g., Who is the author of that book?), another good rule of thumb is to respond to a student's answer with another question that asks for further explanation. Push the kids' thinking as far as you can. It's through such intense reflection that they come to understand concepts at a deeper level. And you will learn so much more when you ask them questions to which you don't already know the answers.

They'll probably resist at first because they won't be used to recognizing and articulating their thought processes. At the beginning, my kids invariably say something like, "I just thinked it in my brain." But don't let them off the hook. Keep at it, coaxing them step by step if necessary, and allow them the time to form their thoughts. They'll get better at it.

"Wait time" is a critical element of teaching for inquiry. Some studies have found that teachers give their students an average wait time of only one second to answer questions. I was amazed to learn this and appalled to realize that I was guilty of doing the same thing. I had to make a very deliberate effort to change this practice, but once I did, I found that my students' contributions to discussions, and the quality of their contributions, increased dramatically. And I found that the implications for assessment were huge. Kids who I had previously considered to be less than stellar students suddenly began to shine—and my expectations for them changed considerably. Thinking takes time; to bring out the best possible thinking from our students, we need to give them that time.

Another useful practice is to challenge their thinking, even when you know they have the "right" answer. For example, if they say they've come up with all the number combinations they can think of to equal six, ask them, "How do you know you have them all?" or something similar. This will force them to dig further and to justify their conclusions—again, leading to higher-level thinking.

Here are some examples of questions you can ask to probe and explore students' thinking and to promote reflection:

- Tell me more about ____.
- What did you do first? Next?
- What made you decide to solve the problem that way?
- Where did you get stuck and what did you do when that happened?
- What did you wonder about when you were working on ____?
- What pictures are you seeing in your mind to help you think about that?

Redirect Students to Each Other

Have you experienced classroom "discussions" which are little more than direct exchanges between you and whatever student happens to be talking (usually one of the same few eager beavers) while the rest of the kids fidget or stare into space? I've certainly been there, many more times than I'd ever want to admit. But I keep trying to work toward the "ideal" discussion, one in which students really listen and talk to each other. The key is redirecting them so they'll have to do this, and there are specific techniques that can help.

First, don't repeat students' answers. This restricts interaction among them because it establishes a limited conversational structure in which every comment has to go through you. It sends a message to the rest of the class that they don't have to listen to each other since the teacher will repeat everything they say anyway.

Instead of repeating what a student said, you can ask that student to say it again—even a third time if necessary—so everyone can hear it. Or ask another student, "Did you hear what Jenny said?" and ask that student to repeat it. You can also go back to the first student and ask, "Is that what you said?" to confirm. Just don't repeat the response yourself.

Another thing you can do is just accept the response without asking for it to be repeated, and ask for further comments from the rest of the class. You'll hear kids asking each other, "What did she/he say?" and repeating the response to each other. Eventually, they'll get the message that you are simply not going to do the work of listening for them, and that the responsibility is theirs.

Of course, it goes without saying that there will be exceptions, perhaps with an exceptionally shy, soft-spoken student or one who has some articulation difficulties. But even in such cases, you can still keep the conversation flowing among the kids by asking them to repeat each others' comments rather than doing so yourself.

Another way of redirecting students to each other, and of promoting their thinking, is to encourage them to agree or disagree. Constance Kamii says, "other people's arguments can cause children to reexamine their own thinking and to construct a higher level of thinking from within" ("Constructivism" 27–28). But the idea is to focus on the content being discussed, not on who's "right" or "wrong." You don't want to set up a competition; what you want is an absorbing intellectual debate. In my class, we do this a lot when the kids are sharing their solutions to math problems, and we call these types of discussions "mathematical arguments." The kids love them and will call for them when there are disagreements. (One year, my first graders were having a difference of opinion about a particular problem, and one of the kids said, "Let's have a mathematical argufight!" The name stuck for the rest of the time we were together.)

Remember the "probe" principle here, however. Once the kids have announced their positions, they need to explain why they think as they do and to try to convince the rest of the class to agree with them. When you make sure the arguments stay focused on the content and that they don't become personal (and you may have to remind the kids of this from time to time), you'll have your students clamoring to share their reasoning and strategies. I can tell you from experience that when a mathematical argument gets going, you stand a very good chance of seeing that "ideal" discussion structure I mentioned earlier. I can't begin to describe what a great feeling it is to suddenly realize that the discussion is going on without you.

Treat Even Routine Procedures and Social Issues Reflectively

The kinds of discussions I'm describing here can and should be a way of life in the classroom, for they stand to help our students develop reflectiveness in every aspect of their lives. When behavioral and social issues arise, utilize the same kinds of questioning techniques to turn the thinking, and the responsibility, back to the children.

Here's a brief example, perhaps not the best, but I hope it will suffice to illustrate this principle. One of my first graders (I'll call him Joey, not his real name), usually a happy little boy, was crying because some of his classmates had noticed a hole in the back of his pants and were staring at it and laughing. I called the class together on the carpet and this dialogue ensued:

> *Me:* How do you think Joey felt when you were all looking at his pants?
>
> *Kids:* Sad.
>
> *Me:* What could you have done instead?
>
> *Mark:* Tape it.
>
> *Kainoa:* Sew it.
>
> *Brittney:* Say nothing.
>
> *Ashley:* Say, "Don't do that to Joey because he won't be your friend."

Me: Should we be nice to him just because he won't be your friend if we're not? (Chorus of "Yes," "No.")

Me: How many of you think we should be nice to him just so he'll be our friend? (About half the class raises hands.)

Me: How many of you think we should be nice to him just because it's the right thing to do? (About half the class raises hands.)

Me: Which do you think is the better reason? (Most seem unsure; no one volunteers an answer.)

Me: Well, let's talk about it some more. What are some other things you could do?

Sandra: Tell him. Say, "Joey, you have a hole in your pants."

Keone: Tape it for him. You could use duct tape.

Nicholas: Call his mom and ask her to get his other pants.

Cynthia: Don't laugh at him.

Elena (rubbing Joey's back): Ask him is he all right.

Keone: Don't tease.

Frank: If Joey says, "Where is the hole?" let him know.

Sandra: Don't take him to show it, just say it's right in back.

Vicky: Think if you laugh it wouldn't feel good to you [if someone laughed at you].

Frank: If we tease him he'd tease us back.

Elena: That wasn't right to do.

Let's examine this conversation more closely. It started because the kids had been unkind to one of their classmates, and it ended with them having a complete change of perspective. How did that happen? I certainly had an agenda and I was clearly leading them, but I spoke only seven times and they spoke sixteen times. You'll notice, too, that most of my utterances were during the first part of the conversation; later, the kids just talked among themselves as they built on each others' ideas.

Years earlier, I would have handled this incident much differently. I'd probably have scolded the kids, telling them why what they were doing was wrong, and ordering them to apologize to Joey. The result would have been an empty, meaningless apology, given only because the teacher demanded it, and the kids would not have learned anything about empathizing with others. This time, I didn't tell them they were wrong. I just asked them questions that required them to think (How do you think Joey felt . . . ?, What could you have done . . . ?, etc.), and they then drew their own conclusions.

Orchestrating the Discourse

Teaching for inquiry requires what the National Council of Teachers of Mathematics calls "orchestrating the discourse" (NCTM, *Professional Standards* 37). You need to know not just what questions to ask, but when to ask them, and even when not to ask them. You need to know which points of a discussion to pick up on and which to leave; when to ask and when to tell; when to listen without commenting and when to enter a discussion; and how to guide the discussion to keep it focused on relevant content and issues. On top of all that, you need to keep in mind that with every interaction, verbal and non-verbal, you send subtle or not-so-subtle messages to your students about what kinds of thinking you value. And to achieve the kind of reflective dialogue you seek, you have to do the thinking yourself; there's no script to follow.

All this takes practice. I tape-record and analyze many of our classroom conversations in order to improve my questioning techniques (I tell the kids what I'm doing and why). I know I'll never be perfect at it, and I still cringe when I hear the opportunities I've missed, but I love the times when things do click. I knew this whole new way of discussion was becoming a habit when I heard the kids tell a new student, as they were pondering a difficult math problem, "She's not going to tell us the answer, you know."

So jump in and keep at it. In time, you'll see a difference in your class discussions and in your kids' attitudes and dispositions toward learning and toward each other, once they come to believe that they are indeed capable thinkers who respect each others' thinking as well. Is it worth doing? Kamii says, "The teacher who protests that he does not have this kind of time because he has a curriculum to cover needs to reexamine his thinking" (*Young Children* 48).

6 Frequently Asked Questions

I n this chapter, I'd like to address some of the questions I'm asked again and again by teachers who are interested in, but uncertain about, an inquiry-based approach.

1. Do we create "real problems," or should we wait for real problems to present themselves?

In an ideal educational world, perhaps we could just wait and go with whatever happens to come up in our classrooms. And with skill and some luck, we'd probably give our students a reasonably solid foundation and a love of learning that might be sufficient for their future endeavors. But the real world, with mandated curriculum and standards galore, is what we're dealing with. And there's worthwhile and necessary knowledge that kids won't ask about simply because they don't have the experience to ask about it—they don't know that they don't know. Besides, I'd hate to think that we didn't know a few more things than our students know! So, while some might disagree with me, I'd say that we can, and should, create opportunities that might not arise naturally. And it doesn't have to be that hard to do.

Do your students need to learn about the history of your area? Bring in an interesting artifact that represents a period they'll need to study about. Leave it out in your room for a few days, let the kids examine it and puzzle over it, and give them time to voice their questions. If they don't start asking, you can start by wondering aloud yourself. Invariably, though, they'll ask about who made or used the item; why, how, and when it was created; and what life might have been like for the people who used it.

Once the questions have started, bring in a collection of fiction and nonfiction books, audio- and videotapes, and other artifacts dealing with that same period, and give the kids time to explore those and generate further questions. Or start with the books, videos, or other resources. Either way, you'll have established a context and jump-started a historical inquiry that has already engaged your students, and you can take it from there as you offer further information, readings, resources, discussions, and experiences.

Some may call it cheating to contrive the start of an inquiry; I don't. It's not the content itself, but the way we go about teaching the content, that makes the difference and supports inquiry. Do we just cover mandated content by having the kids read the textbook, take the end-of-chapter tests, and maybe give a report? Does our approach communicate to our students that we're only teaching this because we have to, because it's in some unfathomable way good for them to know it? Or do we try to find a way to help them become interested in that content, understand it more deeply, and connect it with their lives? The choice is always ours.

2. How do you know when it's time to move on?

It takes some experience and practice, but if you are in tune with your students—that is, truly observing and listening to them—you'll know it's time when you see it. You'll see a difference in the intensity of their engagement when their interest in something starts waning. Their conversations and behavior will be less focused, and you'll wonder if they're ready for something new. That's when you'll have to decide: Is it clearly time to change direction? Or is the topic still so worthwhile that you want them to continue pursuing it? In that case, they might just need a short break, or maybe some redirection, perhaps a little nudge from you in the form of a new question, challenge, or bit of excitement, to get them going again. Then think about what's happening in terms of the Responsive/Reflective Framework (see Figure 3.1): Did they get fired up again? Is it worth it to keep going? Or does it look as if you're just beating the proverbial dead horse?

Teachers are so often expected to cover a program according to its pacing guide that deciding whether to keep going can be unfamiliar and uncomfortable as a result. With inquiry-based planning, these decisions are yours, and they don't come with any publishers' guarantees. But is the alternative—canned, scripted lessons—what you want? Don't worry, just make your best choice and go with it. Over time, you'll get better at it and, believe it or not, you'll eventually become more comfortable with your discomfort. I like the way David and Phyllis Whitin have put it: "in the tension of deciding what to pursue and what to let go, there are not necessarily right or wrong decisions. There are an infinite number of possibilities to pursue, and many are equally fruitful" (*Inquiry at the Window* 124).

3. How do you get kids started thinking and wondering on their own?

This question brings up an issue that troubles me greatly. Kids *always* wonder about things. From birth, they are the quintessential inquirers, as they endeavor to find out about the world around them. They touch and taste everything they can get their hands on, and once they're able to talk, they ask about everything. If you've been with young children at all, you know what I mean.

It's the same when they get to school. I've never had to get kids in the lower elementary grades started wondering on their own. That's exactly what they do! But what happens to them when they get older?

Early in each school year, I ask my students, "What do you wonder about? What is it that you've always wanted to know?" It has saddened me to hear kids from third grade and beyond tell me, "I don't wonder about anything. There's nothing I want to know," while they look at me as if my question, and I, have come from another planet.

Do they really have no questions anymore? Or have they stopped becoming aware of their questions? And if so, why? Do other issues and pressures start to take precedence as kids grow? Do we adults, by selectively reinforcing other behaviors, diminish this drive to know? What turns off that sense of wonder they were born with? What can we do to sustain it, to keep it alive?

We can start by not accepting their responses when they say they don't wonder about anything. I usually answer by looking surprised (because I am) and saying something like, "Everybody wonders about things, no matter how old they are, because there's so much in the world to wonder about; but sometimes we don't pay attention to our wonderings." Because modeling is important, I might share a few of my own questions, but I also emphasize that I'm not expecting their questions to be copies of mine—I want them to share the questions that are really theirs. We talk about the fact that no one can know everything there is to know in the world and that there are no "dumb" questions.

I put up a sheet of chart paper and I invite the kids to start noticing whenever they ask or think of a question about something they'd like to know, and to tell me when that happens so we can post and share their questions (see Figure 6.1). I usually give them time right then to talk with each other in pairs or small groups in order to try to get things started and to make them feel more comfortable about sharing with everyone.

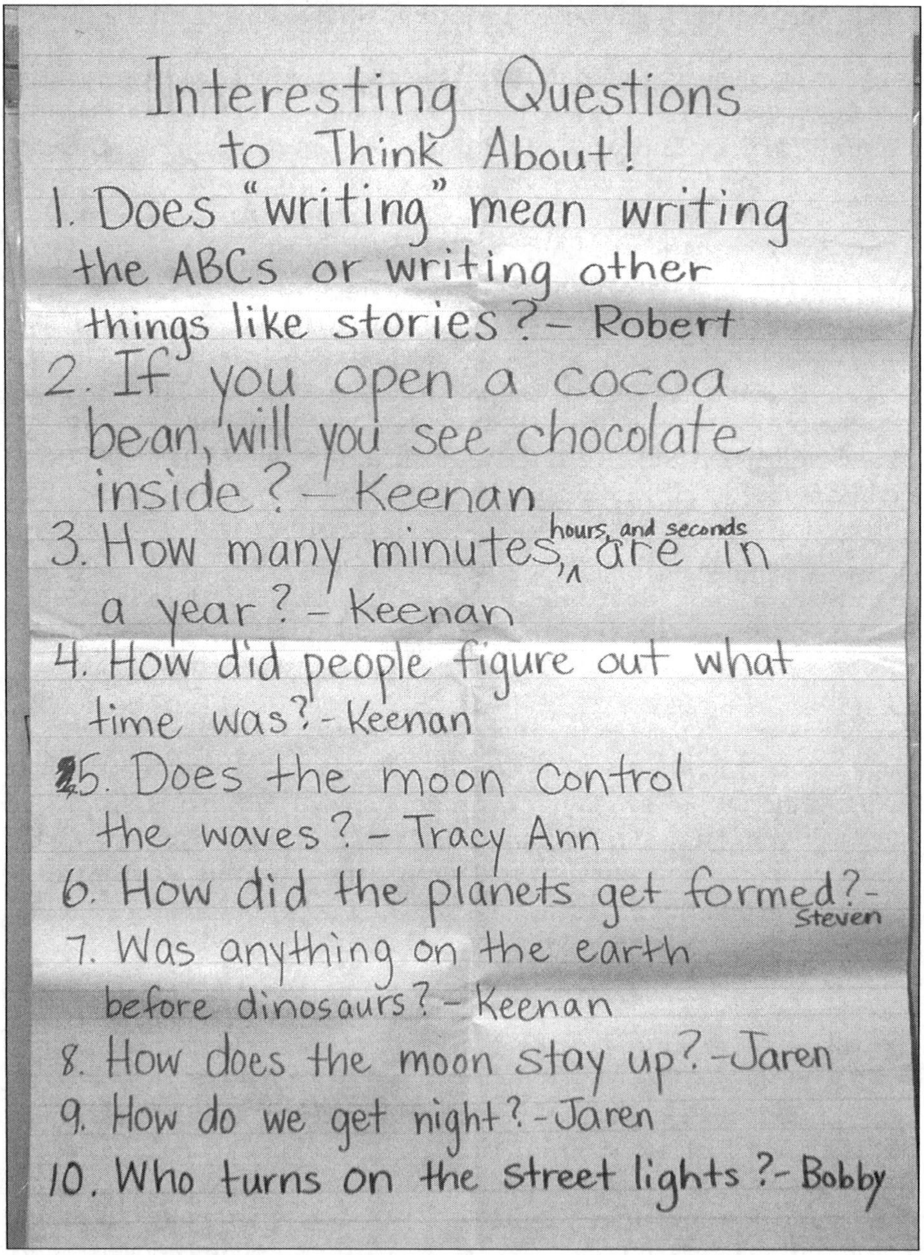

Interesting Questions
to Think About!

1. Does "writing" mean writing
the ABCs or writing other
things like stories? – Robert

2. If you open a cocoa
bean, will you see chocolate
inside? – Keenan

3. How many minutes, hours, and seconds are in
a year? – Keenan

4. How did people figure out what
time was? – Keenan

5. Does the moon control
the waves? – Tracy Ann

6. How did the planets get formed? –
Steven

7. Was anything on the earth
before dinosaurs? – Keenan

8. How does the moon stay up? – Jaren

9. How do we get night? – Jaren

10. Who turns on the street lights? – Bobby

Figure 6.1. Getting inquiry started: an initial Interesting Questions chart.

Sometimes the first question will go up within minutes, and sometimes it will take days. You might even have to help it get started. You might be having a conversation with the class and someone will ask a question, or you might overhear a question being asked in a conversation between students. You can stop them right then and say, "That's an interesting question you just asked. May I write it on the chart so we can share it with everyone?"

It doesn't matter how that first question gets started, or even if it's a question you consider trivial or totally off the wall; what matters is that the process begins, and that the kids start becoming aware of their questions. I guarantee that once things get going, the questions will never stop, as long as you've established the expectation that "in this class, we wonder and we share our wonderings." This is such a big part of what a learning community is all about. You have to live it every day with your kids and you have to believe it. Of course, you'll probably start wondering eventually what kind of monster you've created—you'll be drowning in questions! But when that happens, you can only celebrate and hope that your students' rekindled curiosity will stay with them for the rest of their lives. Society gives a lot of lip service to the term *lifelong learners*, but we don't often think about what that really means. No one can be a true lifelong learner without lifelong questions.

An added thing to be aware of is that inquiry can be expressed in other than verbal ways. Lindfors says, "The question that orients our listening is not 'How come this child doesn't express curiosity about anything?' but rather 'How does this child express his curiosity?'" (66). Learn to look at your kids' faces, read their body language, and be ready to pounce on and respond to whatever sparks of interest you think might be there.

Two books I particularly like to read aloud during these first weeks are *Lizard Sees the World*, by Susan Tews, and *The Wise Woman and Her Secret*, by Eve Merriam. Beyond the considerable enjoyment factor, both of these stories help to develop my students' awareness that there's a whole world out there to wonder about, and they help to legitimize the act of wondering for those who have never thought about it in this way.

4. How far do you go in covering content areas? Are we doing enough? Too much? Too little?

I'll begin this answer with another question: Can you ever learn too much about something? Of course, you want all your kids to be engaged as much as possible in every aspect of their learning, yet they're all individuals. We hear a lot about the need for teachers to differentiate instruction, but inquiry differentiates naturally. Depending on the question or topic being studied, students' levels of interest and involvement will vary. Some kids will leave our classes knowing something about any given area of study, and some will leave as experts who know much more; and that's okay.

So watch your kids and, if you feel they've gained essential understandings but their interest as a whole seems now to be waning, then think about moving on. But—and this is crucial—if one or more students are still totally involved in that inquiry, allow them the time and space to continue pursuing their questions, even if their interest lasts for the rest of the school year. Two of my students spent their entire third- and fourth-grade years researching weather phenomena during every spare moment they could find, including frequent recesses. Three other students in that same class kept up a two-year interest in writing and performing puppet shows. Might the passion they developed for what they were studying be the beginning of their life's work? Who knows? And why should we not encourage such enthusiasm and determination? Whether or not these students will eventually become meteorologists or puppeteers, they were learning how to learn, learning how to be researchers, and learning valuable skills in the process.

5. **How do you manage inquiry-based learning if students have different wonderings, or if their wonderings are not about topics listed in the required curriculum?**

This is tricky, and it took me a long time to work it out for myself. When we encourage inquiry in our classrooms, we usually end up with too many questions, going in so many directions that we don't see how we can ever pull it all together. It becomes so overwhelming that we may give up and revert to pre-planned lessons. But if we're committed to inquiry-based learning, there is a way to manage it and keep our sanity, if we remember a few key principles:

Make time in your schedule for whole-class, small-group, and individual inquiries; there's a need for all of these. The authors of *Learning Together through Inquiry* recommend this type of organization: "We believe in having a class focus because of the depth of inquiry that is possible when students think together within rich supportive contexts. Within this class focus, students pursue individual and small-group inquiries with support from whole-class experiences and from other learners in the classroom" (Short et al. 15).

One semester, I had several small groups of students studying various animals, birds, and insects; one student researching why the

World Trade Center fell; one pair of students trying to find out if there's really a pot of gold at the end of the rainbow; and one group of three students gathering data to answer their burning question, "What's the most popular beginning letter in the dictionary?" All these inquiries were going on simultaneously during time set aside for that purpose, and the kids kept themselves going because they were exploring their own questions. But because they shared their progress regularly during our reflective discussions, they were also aware of and interested in what everyone else was researching; so when they happened upon resources that they thought might be of help to other groups, they made sure to pass the information along.

All this was going on within a whole-class study of Hawaiian history and our ongoing Hidden Places Project. It sounds like a three-ring circus—more than a three-ring circus, I guess—but it worked, because inquiry was an established way of life in our classroom.

If their questions are all over the place, ask the kids to help narrow down the options. I talk with them about the fact that there are different types of questions: Some can't be answered at all through the kinds of research accessible to us; some can be answered in a few minutes by just looking something up; and some can be studied for a lifetime. I then ask them to look through the list of questions we've charted and categorize their questions according to type.

After they've done that, I ask them which types of questions they think would be most interesting and productive to pursue. They usually see that the ones that can be answered quickly, or the ones that can't be answered, would not serve the purpose, so they set those aside and are left with a much more manageable list of beginning possibilities.

From this list of possibilities, try to look at commonalities and work toward consensus. According to David and Phyllis Whitin, "[We] must make choices; some roads must be left untraveled. The danger of losing something potentially fruitful is risky, but in order to proceed, one must take those risks" (*Inquiry at the Window* 122). I would agree; you just can't do everything. So I might say something like, "These are all such interesting questions, but we can't possibly research all of them in the time we have available to us. Do you see some questions that are similar to others in some way? Are there people you might work with whose questions are similar to yours?"

Sometimes the question categories will cluster nicely and you can easily form a manageable number of research groups (I'd suggest starting with no more than four or five groups at a time for an average-sized class). Just as you might do with literature study groups, you can post the list of agreed-upon questions and the kids can sign up for the group they most want to work with. At other times, you might have to limit the choices yourself because there don't seem to be enough commonalities for a natural clustering to occur. When this happens, though, I still leave the door open for individuals to go off in their own directions if their particular questions haven't been included on the list; however, I might ask them to join an ongoing group and save their individual inquiries for a different time of day. It depends on what I know about them and what I hope might be best for them or for the whole class. Again, it's a decision that I, as the teacher, have to make. As with other curricular decisions, I make a choice and go with it; I can always change my decision if, upon reflection, it seems necessary.

Look at kids' individual questions with links to broader understandings in mind. Where are the commonalities that might move your kids toward those understandings? Could their individual or small-group inquiries be carried out and then brought together with your guidance?

Sometimes, the commonalities are fairly obvious already and just need a little push from you to make them evident to your students. One of my first-grade classes sustained an interest in animals for the entire year. Individually and in small groups, they pored over resources to learn and share about the different animals that were their favorites: jaguars, mice, wolves, cheetahs, you name it. In the course of their research, they asked questions that ranged from simple facts ("How big is it?" "Where does it live?") to those that reflected more personal concerns and comparisons with their own family lives ("How do they take care of their babies?" "What do they do when their babies are naughty?" and their favorite, perennial question, "How do they use the bathroom?"). Those more personal questions gave me an opening to guide the kids toward understanding more about the characteristics of animals and humans, the interdependence of life, and so on: all the stuff of the required curriculum. Tying things together in this way also served to unite all the individual, all-over-the-place inquiries with a common thread and to help us move forward with whole-class experiences that were meaningful to everyone.

At other times, you might have to look more deeply to find a meaningful link. One year, my first graders wanted to learn more about space (this was the class that eventually built the stage). They worked with partners to research and share their learning about the planets, stars, and asteroids that intrigued them. That was fine, as far as their experience went at that time, but it wasn't enough. What the kids shared was simply the facts they'd learned. It was up to me and my student teacher, Kim, to help them connect those facts to something larger.

Environmental studies, with a focus on habitats and interdependence, were a major focus of our established first-grade curriculum that year. By thinking of the kids' fact gathering in terms of these larger issues, we came up with a question for them to ponder: "Knowing what you now know about space, which planet would you most like to live on?"

One of the first answers eagerly offered was, "Pluto! That would be so much fun because it has so much snow and ice!" (Well, that does sound exciting to kids who live in Hawai'i!) But immediately, another child said, "But remember, Pluto is so cold that we'd all freeze to death. We couldn't really live there."

Another student said, "Mars would be really neat because it's red, and the sky is red." But then someone responded, "But we wouldn't have any safe water to drink, so we couldn't live there, either."

After several more rounds of discussion (while we charted the conversation), the kids came to what was, for them, a startling realization: Of all the planets in our solar system, Earth is the only one that supports life as we know it, so it's the only planet we could possibly live on—the best and only habitat for us.

We then took it a step further and asked them, "So what does that mean for us on Earth?" As the discussion continued with our guidance, the kids began to understand why it's so critical for us to protect and conserve the resources we have on our planet; we need to take care of the Earth so it will sustain life and take care of us. And, since this was the class that was engaged in the ongoing litter project referred to in Chapter 3 (Example #2), we were able to connect full circle with that investigation.

An interesting side note: A visiting teacher saw the kids' work about space displayed in our classroom and asked us, "How come you're studying about space? That's not part of your first-grade curriculum." We had to explain the connections to her before she was convinced that we weren't total rebels!

But that's the way inquiry works. It really doesn't matter what the particular topics are that kids study, as long as we guide the process and help them make connections to larger concepts and ideas, creating "real problems" and opportunities when necessary (see question #1). We can start anywhere and weave through the curriculum in any number of directions, but we can always get to the required content if we keep working toward important understandings (I keep track to convince myself; you can do the same).

We also need to explain inquiry to parents. They'll usually support our efforts when they understand better what we're doing and why. I try to take advantage of every opportunity to share: in casual conversation, at formal conferences and meetings, and in writing, through homework assignments, dialogue journals, and newsletters (see Appendix 2 for a sample letter).

6. **How do you schedule time for inquiry? What does your day look like? And how can teachers support inquiry if they're bound by mandated curricula and time blocks?**

Let me start by clarifying something. I said earlier that inquiry is not a time of day, it's a way of looking at the world. But realistically, even in the most supportive school setting, no classroom can be a shining model of inquiry every minute of every day. There'll be aspects of your curriculum that won't look or feel like inquiry no matter what, so join the club. We're all human and we'll never achieve that perfect, coherent whole of the "ideal" inquiry-based classroom, even if such an ideal ever could, or should, exist.

So if you're new to all this or if you're allowed only limited time for inquiry in your classroom, don't be afraid to start small, perhaps allowing even one or two short periods each week for your kids to begin exploring whatever their wonderings may be. That may sound contradictory to what I said about inquiry not being a time of day, but I don't mean it to be. You want to establish a certain mindset and process, and you want to keep it manageable so you won't become overwhelmed and give up. Allow yourselves time to grow into it. During these short inquiry times, focus carefully on the kids and reflect often with them and by yourself, using the Responsive/Reflective Framework as your guide. If you do this consistently for a while, the process will begin to extend itself naturally. You and your students will be so energized that you'll want to extend it to other parts of your day, and all you'll have to do is follow and guide it along.

At my school, we have the luxury of mostly uninterrupted classroom time, so we can structure our days as we wish. That, of course, makes as ideal a setting for inquiry-based learning as one could hope for. When you don't have to live by the bell, you can be as flexible as you need to be.

My daily schedule includes large blocks of predictable workshop time. Here's how my "typical" day looks on paper:

> 8:00—Morning routines, chores, settling in
>
> 8:15—Gather in carpet area for morning meeting
>
> 8:45—Writing workshop (whole-class lesson, independent work time, and whole-class sharing/follow-up discussion)

9:40—Recess

10:00—Reading workshop (same format as writing workshop)

10:55—Lunch

11:30—Read-aloud/discussion

12:00—Mathematics workshop (same format as other workshops)

1:00—Other content areas (varies from day to day)

2:00—Dismissal

However, the content and schedule of each day will vary, most often with considerable overlap, depending on what we're immersed in at the time. Our Hidden Places Project, for example, crossed subject-area boundaries, so we didn't confine our scale drawings to "math time" or our caption writing to "writing time"; that would not have made sense, nor would it have been productive. When we worked on that project, we worked on that project, period—and we didn't call it "math" or "writing" time, it was just "work time." Some days we worked on the project for an hour, and sometimes we spent the whole day on it. We didn't work on it every day, but we worked on it often enough to ensure the continuity needed to carry it through.

With inquiry, you need to keep your thinking flexible and keep that Responsive/Reflective Framework in mind. So you planned a math lesson for 12:00, but your kids have just brought up an incredibly profound question about the chapter you've just read aloud, and they're buzzing with excitement, wanting to explore that question. What would you do if you had the choice? Would you cut off their conversation so you could get to the math lesson? Or would you consider giving them time to think about what's uppermost in their minds and save the math for later, even for tomorrow? It all depends on you. You need to decide: Is their literature question worth pursuing? Does it stand to enrich their understanding of the particular story you're reading, of literature in general, of life? Will the world come to an end if you don't do your math lesson at 12:00? Again, there's no right or wrong answer; you watch your kids, make your best guess, and go with it.

Unfortunately, many teachers nowadays have to deal with much more stringent scheduling and curricular constraints. Coping with mandated programs, especially those where everyone in the school has to be doing the same thing in the same time blocks, can be difficult and discouraging. You'll probably have to work around them.

First, can you adjust the way you carry out the packaged curriculum to be at least a little more consistent with your beliefs? Laminack and Ray offer this advice: "We need to ask, 'Are there things in this mandated curriculum I could, with personal modifications, *live with*? Are there any ways I can meet some of the spirit or intent of the mandate without compromising my professional integrity?'" (1). Are there ways you can make inquiry fit within what's required? Perhaps instead of saying to the kids, "That's an interesting question, but sorry, we have to study something else right now," can you think of ways the question might connect with that something else?

Then, think about where you can be most flexible in your scheduling. You might have no choice during the ninety minutes or so each day that you're required to implement the program, but the rest of the day is yours. Use it to find places for inquiry, even small moments, wherever and whenever you can. Who knows, maybe your kids will eventually become such great inquirers and critical thinkers that they'll begin to question what's being done to them by those programs and they'll help us someday to take back our classrooms and our profession. Our kids are our hope for the future. Let's make sure they experience what real learning is about, lest we all forget.

7 Inquiry and Standards (Or, the Soap Box)

One very cold morning during my first year of teaching, I overheard my principal greeting the children as they entered the school. Lewis, one of my kindergartners, burst through the door with his customary great big smile and said, "My hands is cold!" The principal corrected him: "My hands *are* cold!" and Lewis said, "Oh, your hands is cold, too?" That was one of my earliest real-life lessons as a teacher: Just because we've told kids something doesn't mean they've learned what we meant to teach.

I've worked with hundreds of kids since that first year, and the lesson I learned from Lewis is as valid for me today as it was then. As Piaget has said, the child will always answer his own question, but the question that's in his head might not be the same question we thought we were asking. Often, what we perceive as a child's failure to learn is, in reality, our failure to teach.

We're all in agreement that we want to teach our children in the best way we can. But how do we do that? We don't do it by teaching reading, writing, mathematics, or any other subject, and we don't do it by teaching "standards," the standards movement notwithstanding: We do it by teaching *kids*. To put it more accurately, we do it by creating the conditions that will enable kids to learn.

Don't misunderstand what I'm saying. I do care very much about content and student achievement, and about my responsibility to help my students learn what's necessary and important for them. But I don't believe I can help my students achieve anything meaningful if I don't start with them. I have to know them, listen to them, and help them build on what they know by connecting with who they are. Furthermore, I'm convinced that the only way to their minds is through their hearts. And I wouldn't want to impact their minds without impacting their hearts. The world has suffered too much already at the hands of well-educated monsters.

Why their hearts? Why do we teach? We teach to make a difference, for our students as individuals and for the world they will inherit.

Harste says, "curriculum [is] a metaphor for the lives we want to live and the people we want to be" ("What Education as Inquiry" 1).

There's not much point in learning the ABCs unless those letters will be put together to produce thoughts and actions that will make people's lives better. We teach to change the world, one life at a time, in small ways as well as big ones.

Today's political environment can be terribly disheartening to educators. We're bombarded with the so-called "news" that our schools are failing. We hear that the remedy is to test students more, fire teachers and principals, and decrease funding that's already woefully inadequate. And we hear this too often from self-proclaimed "experts" who have no background in education and often no personal stake in the public schools.

This kind of talk drives frightened administrators and teachers to latch onto quick fixes: expensive programs that make elaborate claims and promises, as if children are mindless robots who can and should be programmed to learn the exact same things, in the exact same ways, and at the exact same time.

You and I know there is no truth to that premise. But I fear that in the midst of all the rhetoric and panic, it's the children who will be forgotten, their voices will be lost, and they will indeed be reduced to robots in a self-fulfilling prophecy, unless we can remain true to our beliefs that the children and the future are the reasons we teach.

I believe my role as a teacher is to create a classroom environment that supports and challenges my students as thinkers and learners. I believe, as Dewey said so long ago, that curriculum should be determined through a collaborative process in which both students and teachers have a voice.

As the decision maker in my classroom, I should have the freedom to explore a variety of topics and issues with my children according to how their interests unfold. And along with that freedom, I have the responsibility to help them link their explorations to essential concepts and understandings.

This is the essence of inquiry-based teaching: The particular activities we engage in with our students might vary from class to class, but it's up to us to recognize the possible points of connection with important ideas that each engagement provides and then to help our students make those connections.

Again I cite Dewey, who said that what makes an experience educative is whether conditions are created for further growth in either the same or new directions: "The criterion of the value of school education is the extent in which it creates a desire for continued growth and supplies means for making the desire effective in fact"

(53). This is a crucial distinction, and I try to keep it in mind as I reflect on what's going on with my students: Am I offering them opportunities for thoughtful investigation of questions and issues, or are they simply gathering facts about topics?

And I would take it still further and say that learning must go beyond simply understanding a concept or issue. It must result in action to make the world better. Our classroom learning cycle begins with wondering: "What do I want to know?" followed by intensive research, learning, and sharing what has been learned. But it can't end there, if the point of learning is to make a difference. The ultimate question we ponder is, "What will I do about what I'm learning? Can I do something to make the world better?" If we're learning about pollution, what can I do to help? If we're learning about injustice, what can I do to help? And I don't mean, "What will I do after I'm grown up?" but what can I do right now, as a five- or eight- or ten-year-old kid? Caring and stewardship can be internalized and lived at any age. So our learning cycle continues with action, followed by reflection, more wondering, and on and on—which brings us back to what I said earlier about why we teach, and why we must teach to the heart as well as the mind.

During the two years we were together in grades 3 and 4, my students created—and subsequently revised—a Research Cycle chart (see Figures 7.1 and 7.2). You can see by the new labeling and additional arrows in the revised version how, over time, the kids came to understand the recursiveness of this cycle and the act of wondering as its heart.

We also need to view content with critical thought. A major focal point on my classroom wall is a poster of Albert Einstein, with this quote: "Imagination is more important than knowledge. Knowledge is limited; imagination encircles the world." I placed this poster in a prominent spot, and I ask my students to reflect on it often, because I want it to become an organizing framework for our curriculum. I want my students to think deeply about what constitutes knowledge. I want them to see knowledge as something far beyond the mindless regurgitation of what someone else has determined to be facts. I want them to ask the questions that will drive them to ask more questions. I want them to know that knowledge is a human, continually changing construction, and that they can be not only seekers of knowledge but also creators of knowledge.

Likewise, we need to remember that standards are a human construction, written by adults who have decided what children should know at any given stage in their school years. Standards have not been

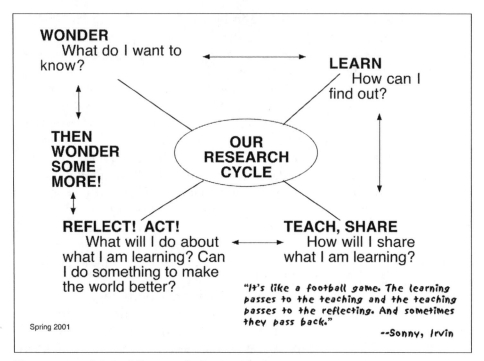

Figure 7.1. Original Research Cycle chart.

handed down on a stone tablet; they are simply the best guesses a particular group of people has made at a particular time for a particular
group of students. And even the best thought-out standards are meant
to be guides, not one-size-fits-all prescriptions. As Joseph Zilliox, University of Hawai'i professor, reminds us, we are talking about "standards, not standardization."

A few more words about standards, so you'll be absolutely clear
about where I stand. I'm okay with standards as a vision of what is
possible—the design and intent of the National Council of Teachers
of English/International Reading Association or the National Council
of Teachers of Mathematics standards, for example. Their standards
documents help me to see essential concepts and connections between
them, and they help me think about my teaching in new ways. But I'm
not okay with standards as a recipe, as they seem mostly to be used
nowadays. Standards were never meant to be checked off one at a time,
nor were they meant to be the starting point for our teaching. I worry
when I hear people say, "Start with the standards," as if teaching were
nothing more than picking a standard, creating a lesson to cover it, and
then picking the next standard. Where are the kids in all this? I've said

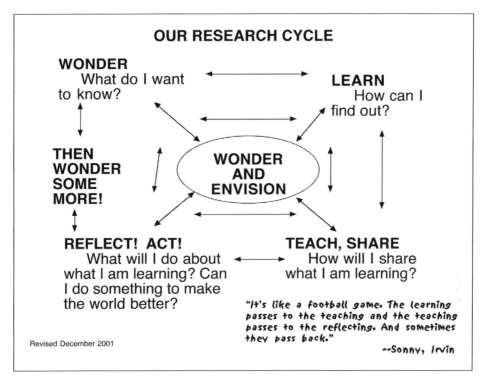

OUR RESEARCH CYCLE

WONDER
What do I want
to know?

LEARN
How can I
find out?

**THEN
WONDER
SOME
MORE!**

**WONDER
AND
ENVISION**

REFLECT! ACT!
What will I do about
what I am learning? Can
I do something to make
the world better?

TEACH, SHARE
How will I share
what I am learning?

*"It's like a football game. The learning
passes to the teaching and the teaching
passes to the reflecting. And sometimes
they pass back."*

--Sonny, Irvin

Revised December 2001

Figure 7.2. Revised Research Cycle chart.

this before and I'll say it again (and I'm not the first or only person to say it): If you want real learning, you can't start with standards; you have to start with learners. If you start with the kids and engage them in a rich learning environment, the standards will emerge and will naturally overlap. Mills, O'Keefe, and Jennings offer this advice: "Our teachers believe that the original intent of the national standards was to give teachers more power and insight, not less. So they use the standards. They don't let the standards use them" (70). See Appendix 3 for an example of keeping inquiry in standards-based lessons.

And that brings me to one more piece of the standards picture, the one I consider most important of all: the idea that standards must be linked with opportunities to learn—access to a quality education—for all our students. That's not the case in every state. Some use the standards as gatekeepers: If you don't measure up, you fail—too bad for you.

We need to believe our students can achieve with our support. We don't write off the kids who come to school without books at home, without the latest designer wear, without a working knowledge of the language of instruction. We don't say, "They can't learn." Instead, we work to find out who they are and what they understand, and we help link their wonderings to those generative educational experiences that will help them move toward, and beyond, achievement of the standards.

My book, *Jamie*, is the story of one of my students and our school experiences together. Jamie was confined to a wheelchair, but she was a remarkably intelligent learner.

In the book, I quote her uncle, who told about a time during Jamie's early therapy when she was given a physical test in which she had to stack a set of blocks. According to the test criteria, she needed to stack at least four blocks in order to pass. And, incredibly, her score would determine whether she was placed in general or special education.

Now you need to know that Jamie had a condition called spinal muscular atrophy, a neuromuscular disease, and she couldn't even hold her head up to see above the second block. Her uncle recalled how angry he was that it took so much time and effort to convince the examiners of the absurdity of holding Jamie to this particular standard (Parker 97).

I think this illustrates exactly what Joe Zilliox means about "standards, not standardization." To have used this test to deny Jamie access to the opportunities afforded by a mainstream education would have been an unforgivable crime. Equity of access is truly a moral issue. The question that should guide us when we make decisions about our students is, "What if this were my child?" If it's not good enough for my child, then it shouldn't be good enough for anyone else's child either.

Diane Stephens says, "I don't care what [trivial facts] you teach each kid; I care that each one is different from having been in your class." We teach to transform lives. Skills alone will never be enough. We need to create in our students a vision of possibilities for themselves and "a disposition to act in the world for the good of others" (Bomer). We do that by being open to possibilities ourselves and seizing them wherever we find them. And the possibilities are always around us, if we develop in ourselves the habit of seeing them.

Epilogue: Vision and Possibilities

So far in this book, I've tried to show how inquiry-based learning works within a whole-class context. But what might it mean for the individuals who make up those classes? I'd like to leave you with one child's story to reflect on.

Aldric

Aldric came to our school and my classroom as a beginning first grader, an extremely capable, but extremely shy, second-language learner. I was told that when he was in kindergarten, some adults had been worried about him because he hardly spoke to anyone.

For a couple of months this continued to be the case. But after a while, Aldric gathered the courage to talk to me one-to-one. One day, he whispered to me that he loved poetry and wanted to become a poet. I invited him to write a poem and share it with me. Here's what he wrote (see Figure E.1):

The Sunny Day

Sunny day, sunny day
I am great,
I feel like a
steaming pot, in
a bathe, I am
hot, in a pot,
whew! that was
really hot,
Ouch!

I asked him if he would share his poem with the class, but he was just too fearful to try. As I said, I need to listen to my students and think about how I can connect their interests with worthwhile educational experiences. I'm not talking just about isolated activities or one-shot deals, but about things that have the potential to become lasting in their lives.

I went home that day realizing that the only way to get Aldric to pursue his dream would be to create a culture of poetry in my classroom. We'd all become poets so Aldric would feel safe enough to find and share his own poetic voice.

Figure E.1. The Sunny Day.

I had studied poetry with my students but had never gotten as deeply into it as I'd wished. Now, Aldric's inquiry became my inquiry, too. I turned to my mentors: professors I study with; author-mentors who guide my teaching; and poets whose work touches me. We began an exploration of poetry that lasted throughout the rest of that school year and the next.

It's strange, but not really strange when you realize how things are connected: As Aldric wrote more poetry, he began to emerge from his shyness and to become a leader in the classroom. Meanwhile, other kids found their voices in poetry, too, as I continued to watch, learn, wonder, and learn some more.

I talked with Aldric a lot about his writing, as I do with all my students. Learning more about their process, about what goes through their heads as they write, helps me understand and teach them better. One day, I asked him how he decides to use certain words in his poems. He said, "I play back the dictionary in my brain and I look for the words I want to use." Isn't that incredible? If I hadn't asked him, I'd never have thought that a six-year-old could already be that intentional in his writing!

Here's another poem Aldric wrote as a second grader (see Figure E.2). Notice the difference in the depth of his thinking and the connection with learning that's important to him:

The Hand

The hand, the hand holds
the pen. The pen, the pen holds
the mind. The mind, the mind
holds the power. The power,
the power holds Mother Earth.

Again, this is the essence of inquiry-based learning. It really doesn't matter that the genre we chose to dwell on was poetry. It could easily have been narrative, non-fiction, or something else entirely. What matters is that through their explorations, the students developed their skills as readers and writers, but with meaning and purpose, with connections to their hearts.

As a teacher, I am the one in control. The decisions are mine to make. But I need to make them with my students in mind. I need to make that connection with them first.

I don't consider Aldric's story a success yet, only a potential success because he has just begun his journey. But I'm hopeful, and I fully expect someday to ask him to autograph his poetry books for me. Aldric can change the world.

Tomorrow

Alfie Kohn is a critic of the "get tough" kinds of standards movements, those that simply exercise more control without more support. He says, "The performance standards set out for schools are frequently offered not as guidelines . . . but as requirements to be imposed on educators.

Figure E.2. The Hand.

The operative word in such discussions is *accountability*, which almost always turns out to mean tighter control over what happens in classrooms by people who are not in classrooms. The effect on learning is comparable to the effect a noose has on breathing" (*What to Look For* 197). What he calls horizontal standards, on the other hand—like those from NCTE/IRA or NCTM—can serve as valuable guiding principles for reconceptualizing teaching and learning. Standards don't have to be a set of increasingly tighter nooses, if we remember that they can help us see a destination, but that only the kids can show us the way to get there.

Never forget that *you* are the decision maker. *You* are the one who makes the critical difference in your classroom. As Stephens and Story say, "I see no substitute for the hard work of understanding a child" (72). By looking at the children first, and by actively pursuing our own professional knowledge in order to guide them, we will have our best chance to help them not only meet the standards but also surpass them beyond our wildest imagination. The students we teach today will become our guides as they create the world, and the standards, of tomorrow.

Appendix 1: Responsive/Reflective Lesson Planning Worksheet

This section may be reproduced for your use. It can be enlarged to 8 1/2" × 11" size by setting your photocopier enlarger to approximately 120 percent.

Step 1. What do you notice?
Things to consider: What is happening with the students that you might build upon? What classroom events are occurring? What books are the students enjoying? What questions are they asking? What interests are they demonstrating? How do you know?

Step 2. Response: What are some possibilities for building on what you notice?
Things to consider: How might you turn some aspect of Step 1 into a worthwhile educational experience? Consult your standards and other resources and brainstorm some ideas.

Step 3. Choose one idea from Step 2 and develop it further.
Things to consider: What could you have the children do? How will it connect with Step 1 or with previous things they've done? How will it connect with your school's required content and standards?

Step 4. Afterward: Reflection
Things to consider: What happened? How do you feel about it? How do the children feel about it? Was this experience meaningful to them? Did it challenge their thinking? How do you know? What do you think they learned? How do you know? What did *you* learn? What might you do differently next time?

Step 5. Possibilities
Things to consider: What possibilities, if any, do you see for extending this experience further? Go back to Step 1 and brainstorm some ideas.

Appendix 2: Helping Families Support Inquiry: A Sample Letter

One challenge with inquiry-based learning is helping parents to understand our curriculum. I believe in communicating with them from the beginning of the school year, before they ask questions, rather than waiting and hoping they won't ask. We want parents to be our allies and to support their children's inquiries at home, and I've found that the more we share, the more that is likely to happen.

The end of the school year is also an important time to share. Here's a letter I wrote for our PTA's newsletter, just before the kids left for summer vacation:

Dear Waikele Elementary Families,

When vacation approaches, parents often ask, "What can I do to support my child's learning during the summer?" Reading to and with your child, visiting the library often, and taking family outings together are all very important, but you've probably heard that advice many times before. So we'd like to focus this list on some ideas that are in keeping with our school's philosophy: how you can support your child as an inquirer.

At Waikele, our curriculum supports inquiry-based learning. We teach what is required, but within the required content, we encourage children to explore questions about things they *want* to know, and we help them connect what they find out to what they *need* to know. By pursuing the questions that really matter to them, they'll be more involved in their learning and will become more independent learners.

For example, kids are often curious about animals. As teachers, we might help them learn how to find and share information about specific animals they're interested in. But it doesn't matter which animals they choose, because we'll help them connect the facts they learn about those animals to larger ideas, such as how animals and humans depend on each other. Our goal is to

help them understand more about their own roles and responsibilities within their families, community, and world. And in the
process, we help them learn the skills and strategies they need to
be researchers of anything.

So what can parents do this summer to support their children
as inquirers? We offer these suggestions:

- *Encourage your child's questions.* Sometimes kids ask so many
  questions that we can lose sight of the fact that this is a good
  thing. If it's a busy time, ask them to wait a few minutes
  until you're available to listen. Not every question can be
  answered, but we always want to encourage our children
  to wonder. If we don't ask questions, we don't learn.

- *Ask your child questions that show your interest.* Ask things
  like, "What made you think of that?" "Why is that important (or interesting) to you?" "How do you think you
  might find out?"

- *Be an inquirer yourself, and a co-learner with your child.* You
  don't have to know the answers to the questions your
  child asks. You might say something like, "I wonder about
  that myself. How do you think we could find out?" and
  then look for answers together. When you show a genuine
  excitement for learning, your child will see that learning is
  lifelong.

- *Be a listener and guide,* but don't be too quick to take over
  if your child encounters some difficulty in the search.
  Use your judgment about when to step in. Carolyn Burke,
  a well-known educator, says, "Don't step in front of the
  struggle; if you step in front of the struggle, you take away
  the learning" (quoted by Whitin).[1]

- *Help your child gain access to needed resources.* This doesn't have
  to cost money. You can help your child to visit the library,
  access the Internet, or contact experts for information. You
  can provide time, space, and possibly some "around-the-
  house" materials to support your child's inquiry.

- *Respect your child as a thinker and learner.* Children have different strengths and learn in different ways. By support-
  ing our children's inquiries, we might even be helping
  them to find lifetime careers or interests. Tomie dePaola,

---

1. Burke, Carolyn (qtd. by Whitin, David). "Language and Mathematics: Partners for
Learning." National Council of Teachers of English Conference. Moscone Convention
Center, San Francisco. 21 Nov. 2003.

a popular children's author/illustrator, says that he was always drawing when he was a child (even when he wasn't supposed to be drawing), and that his parents encouraged this by providing him with the drawing materials he needed. Today, readers are enjoying over 150 of his books, with more to come!

- *Reflect and continue the inquiry process with your child.* Ask questions such as, "What do you think about what you found out?" "Did anything surprise you?" "What do you wonder about now?" Questions such as these will help your child understand that learning is continuous. And be sure to share your own reflections so that your child will see that your learning goes on, too.

Have a wonderful summer and enjoy being an inquirer and researcher with your child!

Appendix 3: Keeping Inquiry in Standards-Based Lessons

As our Hawai'i school system now requires all lessons to be standards-based, a dilemma has resulted for those of us wishing to preserve inquiry-based learning: How can we write standards-based lesson plans that will still maintain the integrity of our beliefs? I had to submit such plans as a requirement for several district workshops, and so far (four years after the fact), I haven't had them returned to me as "wrong" (of course, I have no idea if anyone ever really read them)! I share two of those plans here as examples, with the hope that they'll be helpful if your school or district is demanding such plans from you. These are based on our state standards, but you could easily insert your own local standards within the plans you create.

Sample Lesson Plan #1 (Grade 4)

Explanatory Notes

This lesson is meant to be the beginning of a semester-long inquiry into poetry. The inquiry will include author and craft studies as well as the writing of poetry. My goal is for my students to find themselves in poetry and to make poetry a part of their lives.

Throughout the inquiry, students will explore poetry on three levels:

- Reading and enjoying poetry;
- Making deep personal connections with poetry;
- Analyzing the craft of poetry.[1]

---

1. Heard, Georgia. *For the Good of the Earth and Sun.* Portsmouth, NH: Heinemann, 1989.

Students will be learning to write poetry by studying the work of various poets through the following "reading like a writer" inquiry process, with which they're already familiar:

1. *Notice* something about the craft of the text.
2. *Talk* about it and *make a theory* about why a writer might use this craft.
3. Give the craft a *name*.
4. Think of *other texts* you know. Have you seen this craft before?
5. Try to *envision* using this crafting in your own writing (Ray 120).[2]

In keeping with my inquiry-based curriculum, I've chosen to use my own lesson plan format. I've attached an explanation of this format, followed by the lesson plan itself. [I attached a copy of the Responsive/Reflective Lesson Planning Framework.]

Poetry Inquiry: Exploring Poetry

1. *What do you notice?*

Students have engaged in sustained craft studies of memoir and nonfiction during this school year. They are beginning to internalize the "reading like a writer" process that has characterized these studies.

My students found much personal meaning as they wrote their memoirs during the first semester. Several have now begun to show an interest in poetry.

2. *What are some possibilities for building on what you notice?*

A focused inquiry into poetry seems a natural next step to help my students continue to find personal meaning in reading and writing and to extend their knowledge of various genres. Studying the craft of poetry can also help build on our ongoing exploration of "amazing words."

3. *Choose one idea and develop it further.*

My main purpose for this lesson is to gain some insight into my students' current understandings of and attitudes toward poetry and to initiate the inquiry process.

---

2. Ray, Katie Wood. *Wondrous Words*. Urbana, Illinois: National Council of Teachers of English, 1999.

1. Discuss and chart students' initial thoughts:

   - What is a poem?

   - What do you know about poetry?

   - How do you feel about poetry?

2. Do a brief book talk to introduce the collection of poetry books gathered to begin this inquiry. Give students time to explore these books. Observe, listen, and interact with them, recording any observations that might be useful for follow-up discussions and lessons.

3. Debrief with whole class, charting their thoughts and theories and discussing any generalizations and/or questions that might emerge:

   - What did you notice about the poems you explored?

   - What did you like/not like?

   - What surprised you?

   - What do you wonder about?

   - Why might writers want to write poetry?

Standards

This inquiry will address several standards, both simultaneously and over time. These standards will encompass both reading and writing as they connect and overlap. Because this lesson is an initial exploration, it will focus mainly on the following reading content standard:

- Range: Read a range of literary and informative texts for a variety of purposes.

The benchmark this lesson most closely addresses is as follows:

- (Gr. 4–5): Read for literary experience and to develop aesthetic appreciation.

Assessment

I will assess students' initial understandings by looking at their contributions to the group discussions (evidence will be on charts and in my notes) and by observing, listening to their conversations, and interacting with them as they explore the poetry books. (Next lesson: Making personal connections with poetry.)

Sample Lesson Plan #2 (Grade 4)

In keeping with my inquiry-based curriculum, I've chosen to use my own lesson plan format. I've attached an explanation of this format, followed by the lesson plan itself. [I attached a copy of the Responsive/Reflective Lesson Planning Framework.]

Personal Writing: A Letter to the President

1. *What do you notice?*

Students have just completed taking the state test and reflecting on the experience. We discussed the new federal law that has made yearly testing mandatory for all students. Our discussion brought out the many strong emotions students had in response to the test.

2. *What are some possibilities for building on what you notice?*

I think the students need to address this issue more thoroughly. I hope that writing about it in a more personal way will help them do just that.

3. *Choose one idea and develop it further.*

I plan to ask them to write a letter to the president sharing their thoughts about this law. This is the assignment:

President Bush has made a law that all students have to be tested every year, beginning in third grade. He says that these tests are the only way to find out if students are learning.

Write a letter to President Bush telling him what you think about this law. You might write about these things:

- Do you think the law is fair? Why or why not?

- Does the test show everything you're learning?

- Is the test the only way to show what you're learning? Are there any other ways to show what you're learning?

- If you were the president, would you change the law or keep it? Why?

- What else do you want to tell or ask the president?

Be polite and respectful, but be honest about how you feel. Your voice is important!

Standards

This lesson will focus mainly on the following writing content standard:

- Range: Write using various forms to communicate for a variety of purposes and audiences.

The benchmark I am looking at is:

- (Gr. 4–5): Write to communicate information, express opinions, and influence others.

Assessment

I will assess the students' writing using the Hawai'i Writing Assessment, the state language arts standards, and our own classroom rubric (developed with the students) as my guides.

The assessment tool I will use is the Hawai'i Writing Assessment's rubric for meaning.

Bibliography

Ball, Deborah Loewenberg. "What's All This Talk About 'Discourse'?" *Arithmetic Teacher* 39 (1991): 44–48.

Berghoff, Beth, Kathryn A. Egawa, Jerome C. Harste, and Barry T. Hoonan. *Beyond Reading and Writing: Inquiry, Curriculum, and Multiple Ways of Knowing.* Urbana, IL: Whole Language Umbrella & National Council of Teachers of English, 2000.

Bomer, Randy. "Reading: So What?: Relationships between Reading and Social Action." National Council of Teachers of English Conference. Colorado Convention Center, Denver. 19 Nov. 1999.

Cambourne, Brian. *The Whole Story: Natural Learning and the Acquisition of Literacy in the Classroom.* New York: Ashton Scholastic, 1988.

Carle, Eric. *The Tiny Seed.* New York: Simon & Schuster, 1987.

Cazden, Courtney. *Classroom Discourse: The Language of Teaching and Learning.* Portsmouth, NH: Heinemann, 1988.

Crews, Donald. *Shortcut.* New York: William Morrow, 1996.

Dewey, John. *Democracy and Education: An Introduction to the Philosophy of Education.* 1916. New York: The Free Press, 1966.

Duckworth, Eleanor. *The Having of Wonderful Ideas.* New York: Teachers College Press, 1996.

Goodman, Yetta. "Kidwatching: An Alternative to Testing." *National Elementary School Principal* 47 (1978): 41–45.

Harste, Jerome C. "Inquiry-Based Instruction." *Primary Voices K–6* 2 (1993): 2–5.

———. "What Education as Inquiry Is and Isn't." *Critiquing Whole Language and Classroom Inquiry.* Ed. Boran, Sibel, and Barbara Comber. Urbana, IL: National Council of Teachers of English, 2001. 1–17.

Kamii, Constance. "Constructivism and Beginning Arithmetic (K–2)." *Teaching and Learning Mathematics in the 1990s.* Ed. Cooney, Thomas, and Christian Hirsch. Reston, VA: National Council of Teachers of Mathematics, 1990. 22–30.

———. *Young Children Reinvent Arithmetic.* New York: Teachers College Press, 1985.

Kohn, Alfie. *Beyond Discipline: From Compliance to Community.* Alexandria, VA: Association for Supervision and Curriculum Development, 1996.

———. *What to Look For in a Classroom.* San Francisco: Jossey-Bass, 1998.

Labinowicz, Ed. *The Piaget Primer.* Menlo Park, CA: Addison Wesley, 1980.

Laminack, Lester, and Katie Wood Ray. "Message from the Editors." *Primary Voices* 9.3 (2001): 1–2.

Lankshear, Colin, and Peter McLaren. *Critical Literacy: Politics, Praxis, and the Postmodern.* Albany, NY: SUNY Press, 1993.

Lindfors, Judith. *Children's Inquiry: Using Language to Make Sense of the World.* New York: Teachers College Press; Urbana, IL: National Council of Teachers of English, 1999.

Merriam, Eve. *The Wise Woman and Her Secret.* New York: Simon and Schuster, 1991.

Mills, Heidi, Timothy O'Keefe, and Louise B. Jennings. *Looking Closely and Listening Carefully: Learning Literacy through Inquiry.* Urbana, IL: National Council of Teachers of English, 2004.

National Council of Teachers of English and International Reading Association. *Standards for the English Language Arts.* Urbana, IL: National Council of Teachers of English; Newark, DE: International Reading Association, 1996.

National Council of Teachers of Mathematics. *Principles and Standards for School Mathematics.* Reston, VA: National Council of Teachers of Mathematics, 2000.

———. *Professional Standards for Teaching Mathematics.* Working draft. Reston, VA: National Council of Teachers of Mathematics, 1989.

Parker, Diane. *Jamie: A Literacy Story.* Portland, ME: Stenhouse, 1997.

———. "Take Care of Mother Earth: Technology and the Environment." *Teaching Children Mathematics* 9 (2003): 414–419.

Ray, Katie Wood. *Wondrous Words.* Urbana, IL: National Council of Teachers of English, 1999.

Schwartz, Sydney. "Hidden Messages in Teacher Talk: Praise and Empowerment." *Teaching Children Mathematics* 2 (1996): 396–401.

Short, Kathy, Jerome Harste, and Carolyn Burke. *Creating Classrooms for Authors and Inquirers.* 2nd ed. Portsmouth, NH: Heinemann, 1995.

Short, Kathy G., Jean Schroeder, Julie Laird, Gloria Kauffman, Margaret J. Ferguson, and Kathleen Marie Crawford. *Learning Together through Inquiry: From Columbus to Integrated Curriculum.* Portland, ME: Stenhouse, 1996.

Snicket, Lemony. *The Bad Beginning.* New York: HarperCollins, 1999.

Stephens, Diane. "When Accountability Becomes Responsibility: Stories from Empowered Teachers Who Are Making a Difference." National Council of Teachers of English Conference. Colorado Convention Center, Denver. 23 Nov. 1999.

Stephens, Diane, and Jennifer Story, eds. *Assessment as Inquiry.* Urbana, IL: National Council of Teachers of English, 2000.

Tews, Susan. *Lizard Sees the World.* New York: Clarion Books, 1997.

Vygotsky, Lev. *Mind in Society: Development of Higher Psychological Processes.* Cambridge, MA: Harvard University Press, 1978.

Watson, Ken, and Bob Young. "Discourse for Learning in the Classroom." *Language Arts* 63 (1986): 126–133.

Wells, Gordon. *The Meaning Makers.* Portsmouth, NH: Heinemann, 1986.

Wells, Gordon, and Gen Ling Chang-Wells. *Constructing Knowledge Together.* Portsmouth, NH: Heinemann, 1992.

Whitin, Phyllis, and David Whitin. *Inquiry at the Window.* Portsmouth, NH: Heinemann, 1997.

———. *Math Is Language Too.* Urbana, IL: National Council of Teachers of English; Reston, VA: National Council of Teachers of Mathematics, 2000.

With Hope for the Future . . .

My mom, Celia Fichman, was an elementary school teacher from the early 1950s to the 1970s. At her retirement celebration in 1973, her colleagues shared this story as her administrators presented her with a Meritorious Service Award:

> Our school is well known for innovative programs, and the key word is flexibility. A decade ago, our principal introduced a new reading program to our school.
>
> Secure in the knowledge that the new program was functioning well, the principal invited the superintendent and other district administrators to drop in any time and see the program in motion.
>
> The visitors popped into Cel's classroom unannounced at the time the reading lesson was scheduled. To their delight, instead of the reading lesson, they found the class involved in a science demonstration. Cel and her pupils were watching a pigeon laying eggs on the window sill.

May our children, and the teachable moment, always matter.

Author

Diane Parker has been an elementary school teacher in Connecticut and Hawai'i and is presently a part-time faculty member of the University of Hawai'i College of Education, working with preservice teachers and their mentors during their classroom field experiences. She is the author of *Jamie: A Literacy Story* and several articles published in educational journals. Since she has retired from full-time teaching, she is also enjoying her new opportunities to travel more frequently with her husband, exercise more regularly, and meet friends for coffee or brunch on weekday mornings without feeling as if she's playing hooky from school.

This book was typeset in Palatino and Helvetica by Precision Graphics.
Typefaces used on the cover were Americana and Palatino.
The book was printed on 60-lb. White Williamsburg Offset paper by Versa Press, Inc.